Leveled Text-Dependent Question Stems

Social Studies

What information is not provided in the text?

How does this map show changes in _____?

Tell the text's events in the order they happened.

Use details from the text to describe the cause of _____.

How are the central messages of the texts similar? How are they different?

What is the author's purpose in creating this image?

Identify the main point of the text. Cite details the author...

What inferences/interpretations can you make from the...

How are the central messages of the texts similar? K...

What does the author want you to understand about _____

Based on what you read about _____

How is _____

What evidence is there that the author...

Describe the difference between...

Author

Niomi Henry, Ed.S.

SHELL EDUCATION

Contributing Author

Jodene Lynn Smith, M.A.

Publishing Credits

Corinne Burton, M.A.Ed., *President*; Conni Medina, M.A.Ed., *Managing Editor*; Emily R. Smith, M.A.Ed., *Content Director*; Lee Aucoin, *Senior Graphic Designer*; Lynette Ordoñez, *Editor*; Stephanie Bernard, *Assistant Editor*

Image Credits

p.15 Library of Congress [LC-USZ62-7816]; p.111 The Granger Collection; p.125 Library of Congress [ar171300]; p.127 pm001305; p.133 Library of Congress [LC-USE6-D-002275; p.135 Library of Congress [LC-USZC4-6262]; p.137 Library of Congress [LC-US2c4-1128]; p.139 Library of Congress [LC-US262-51821]; all other images Shutterstock and iStock Images

Standards

© Copyright 2010. National Governors Association Center for Best Practices and Council of Chief State School Officers. All right reserved.

© 2007 Board of Regents of the University of Wisconsin System. World-Class Instructional Design and Assessment (WIDA)

Shell Education

A division of Teacher Created Materials
5301 Oceanus Drive
Huntington Beach, CA 92649-1030
www.tcmpub.com/shell-education
ISBN 978-1-4258-1646-9
© 2017 Shell Educational Publishing, Inc.

Table of Contents

What Are Text-Dependent Questions?

From literary novels and dramas, to textbooks, word problems, newspaper articles, scientific reports, primary sources, and websites, texts vary in content and style. Regardless of the format, students must be able to decode and comprehend the contents of the texts to learn from the material. Text-dependent questions (TDQs) increase students' understanding through in-depth examinations of particular aspects of the texts. They guide students to examine specific portions of the texts and then provide evidence for their answers. Unlike other types of questions, TDQs rely solely on the text so that students may not necessarily need to access significant background knowledge or include outside information.

TDQs facilitate the comprehension of text on a variety of levels. On the most specific level, these questions help students analyze words and sentences within the text to determine the specific meanings and connotations of particular words and phrases. TDQs also enable students to study broader concepts, such as text structure and point of view. They aid students in their study of the individuals, settings, and sequences of events in a text and provide a means for investigating the presence of other types of media within the writing (e.g., drawings, illustrations, graphs, tables). These questions offer an effective tool for helping students analyze the overarching themes, concepts, arguments, and claims presented in texts. TDQs help students build their abilities to compare multiple texts to each other on a variety of topics. Through thoughtful design and sequencing, TDQs can be tailored to meet many specific educational standards and learning objectives while still maintaining a direct connection to the text.

Leveled Text-Dependent Questions

Leveling TDQs helps teachers differentiate content to allow all students access to the concepts being explored. While the TDQ stems are written at a variety of levels, each level remains strong in focusing on the content and vocabulary presented in the texts. Teachers can focus on the same content standard or objective for the whole class, but individual students can access the texts at their independent instructional levels rather than at their frustration levels.

Teachers can also use the TDQs as scaffolds for teaching students. At the beginning of the year, students at the lowest reading levels may need focused teacher guidance as they respond to the questions. As the year progresses, teachers can begin giving students multiple levels of the same questions to aid them in improving their comprehension independently. By scaffolding the content in this way, teachers can support students as they move up through the thinking levels.

What Are Text-Dependent Questions? *(cont.)*

Creating TDQs

This book offers 480 of text-dependent question stems that can be used to increase reading comprehension in social studies. Each question stem can be slightly altered to ask the type of question you need. However, it may be necessary to create other TDQs to supplement or support the ones supplied in this book.

When considering what type of TDQ to ask, it is important to think about the key ideas in the text and the desired outcomes of the lesson. What should students understand at the end of the lesson? What are the core concepts of the text? Once these main ideas and objectives have been identified, teachers can determine the particular aspects of the text that should be studied for students to reach these goals. Examine key vocabulary words and important text structures that are related to the underlying core concepts, and develop questions that highlight these connections. Furthermore, identify complex sections of the text that may prove difficult for students, and create questions that allow students to address and master the comprehension challenges presented by the text.

It is also important to consider the sequence of the TDQs presented to students. Generally, the opening questions should be straightforward, giving students the opportunity to become familiar with the text and removing any technical obstacles, such as challenging vocabulary words, which could hinder comprehension. After students gain a basic understanding of the text, introduce more complex questions that strive to illuminate the finer, more intricate concepts. By scaffolding the questions to move from basic, concrete topics to elaborate, implied concepts, you can use TDQs to guide students to a detailed understanding of the complexities of a text.

The key to making sure that questions are dependent on the text is to think about the answer. Can the answer be found in the text, or is an inference created based on facts in the text? If the answer is anchored to the text in some way, it is a strong TDQ!

Setting the Stage for Text Analysis

When using questioning strategies for text analysis, it is vital to establish a safe and collaborative classroom environment. TDQs are designed to stimulate critical-thinking skills and increase reading comprehension in all content areas. It is building these skills, not getting the "right answer," that is the ultimate goal, and students may need to be reminded of this fact. Many TDQs are open ended and don't have single, correct answers. To ensure a collaborative classroom environment, students need to be confident that their answers to questions and their contributions to classroom discussions will be respected by everyone in the room.

TDQs Across the Content Areas

It is usually regarded as the task of the English or language arts teacher to guide students through the effective use of comprehension strategies as they read. Although students read in almost every subject area they study, some teachers may overlook the need to guide students through comprehension tasks with textbooks, primary sources, or nonfiction pieces. Comprehension strategies best serve students when they are employed across the curricula and in the context of their actual learning. It is only then that students can independently use the strategies successfully while reading. Students will spend the majority of their adulthoods reading nonfiction expository writing. With this in mind, teachers at all levels must actively pursue ways to enhance their students' abilities to understand reading material. Utilizing TDQs specific to social studies content is one way to achieve this goal.

TDQs can be used to facilitate the comprehension and understanding of any type of text. These strategies can, and should, be applied to any type of text across disciplines and content areas. For example, text-based primary sources, such as letters and speeches, provide excellent opportunities for the use of TDQs in the social studies classroom. Biographies and autobiographies of historical figures offer ample opportunity for in-depth study through TDQs as well.

Twenty-First Century Literacy Demands

The literacy demands of the twenty-first century are tremendous. Literacy was defined a century ago by one's ability to write his or her own name. In the 1940s, one needed to be able to read at the eighth-grade level to function adequately in the factory setting. To be considered literate today, one needs to be able to read text written at high school levels as a part of workplace and civic duties and leisure activities.

Students and teachers today have entered a new era in education—one that is deeply tied to the technological advances that permeate the modern world. Today, some children can use cell phones to take pictures before they learn to talk. Students in school use the Internet and online libraries to access information from remote locations. Now more than ever, it is the content-area teacher's responsibility to prepare students for the diverse and rigorous reading demands of our  technological age. To become effective and efficient readers, students must utilize comprehension strategies automatically and independently. Students need teacher guidance to help them become independent readers and learners so that they not only understand what they read but also question it and explore beyond it.

TDQs Across the Content Areas *(cont.)*

Integrating Literacy and Social Studies

The goal of literacy in social studies is to develop students' curiosity about people and the world around them and to promote effective citizenry in a culturally diverse world. Studying relationships among people and between people and the environment helps students make better sense of the world in which they live. Another important goal of literacy in social studies is to introduce students to the idea of looking at the world and current issues through specific lenses: historical, economic, civic, and geographical. To accomplish these goals, students must learn how to closely study and reflect on various social, economic, cultural, religious, and geographical topics. Students must also learn how to support their thinking with evidence from the texts they're reading. With these skills well in hand, students can understand the complexity of available information, are empowered to become independent learners, and learn to consider perspectives that they might otherwise overlook.

Using Primary and Secondary Sources

Every day, people create and use primary sources that leave clues about their lives and about the workings of governments or businesses. These items include personal papers, letters, notes, photographs, maps, drawings, newspapers, government documents, and more. To be a legitimate primary source, someone who observed an event or period in history must authentically create the item about that topic. A person watching a battle can write a primary source newspaper article about it. Someone who hears about the battle through the Associated Press wire and writes an article to describe it is actually creating a secondary source. Items such as textbooks and biographies of historical figures are also secondary sources. Both primary and secondary sources and texts are valuable tools in teaching social studies.

Primary sources add real-life connections to social studies. Through primary sources, students walk in the shoes of those who lived before them. They can also begin to understand their own ties to the past. Secondary sources can explain information, facts, and details in a historically significant manner. Authors may present multiple perspectives of the same event and offer their own insights and research on the topic. Students should consider an author's perspective and reasons for writing when analyzing either primary or secondary sources.

Note
Throughout this book, the term *text* is used in the leveled text-dependent question stems to refer to informational texts, documents, photographs, maps, posters, charts, and so on. When presenting the questions to students, teachers should substitute the specific type of text for that word. The examples illustrate how to do this.

Skills and Descriptions

Literacy-Based Skill	Description	Page
Understanding People, Places, Events, and Concepts	Students have a basic understanding of the people, places, events, and concepts in a text to support deeper analysis of the text.	10
Identifying Key Details and Facts	Students identify key details and facts in a text that are relevant to the topic or historical context.	22
Summarizing Positions	Students identify positions presented in a text and summarize them using the most relevant information from the text.	34
Interpreting Content	Students use a variety of strategies to interpret content in a text and deepen their understanding of the event or time period.	46
Inferring	Students combine a variety of strategies with information from the text to draw conclusions.	58
Analyzing Perspectives	Students identify and analyze perspectives presented in a text and consider events or ideas that can affect one's perspective.	70
Analyzing Change and Continuity	Students study chronology and cause and effect as they analyze how past events unfolded and how they affect later events.	82
Comparing and Contrasting	Students identify similarities and differences between people, places, events, time periods, and concepts.	94
Evaluating Texts	Students conduct critical analyses of a text to make judgments about an idea or assess an author's claim or evidence.	106
Maps, Graphs, and Charts	Students understand and analyze primary- and secondary-source maps, graphs, charts, and their features.	118
Artwork, Photographs, and Posters	Students apply social studies literacy skills to artwork, photographs, and posters.	130
Connecting Texts	Students use social studies literacy skills to make connections between texts.	142

How to Use This Book

Skill Overview—Each skill is defined on the first page of its section. This explains what the skill is and how to introduce it to students.

Complexity—The text-dependent question stems in this book are differentiated to four complexity levels. The levels roughly correlate to four grade ranges as follows:

- ☆ grades K–1

- ◯ grades 2–4

- ▢ grades 5–8

- △ grades 9–12

Implementing the Question Stems—The second page of each section contains an example question stem differentiated to all four complexity levels. This is a great way for teachers to see a model of how the leveled text-dependent questions can be used with their students.

Question Stems—Each of the 12 sections includes 10 question stems differentiated to four complexity levels for a total of 480 questions in the book. Along with a chart showing the 10 question stems, each complexity level also includes a leveled passage with sample text-dependent questions.

K–12 Alignment—The final two pages in each section include the leveled text-dependent question stems in one chart. This allows teachers to use these two pages to differentiate the text-dependent questions for their students.

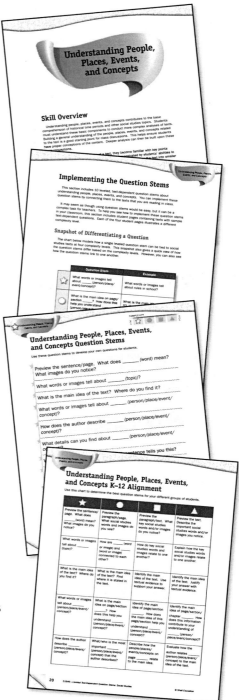

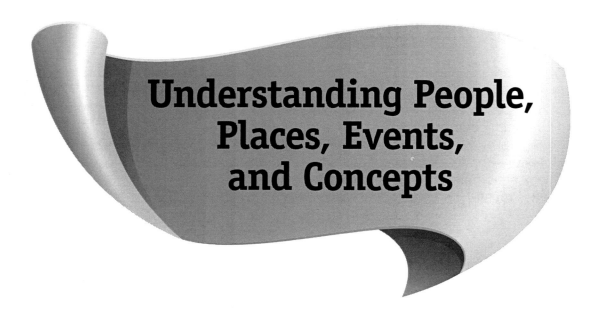

Understanding People, Places, Events, and Concepts

Skill Overview

Understanding people, places, events, and concepts contributes to the basic comprehension of historical time periods and other social studies topics. Students must understand these basic components to conduct more complex analyses of texts. Building a general understanding of the people, places, events, and concepts related to the text is a good starting point for class discussions. This helps ensure that students have proper understandings of the content. Deeper analysis can then be built upon these basic understandings.

As students build understanding of a text, they become familiar with key points and details of the text. Comprehension can be demonstrated by students' abilities to decode the text at the sentence and/or paragraph level. Breaking the text into smaller sections also provides additional support for students who need it.

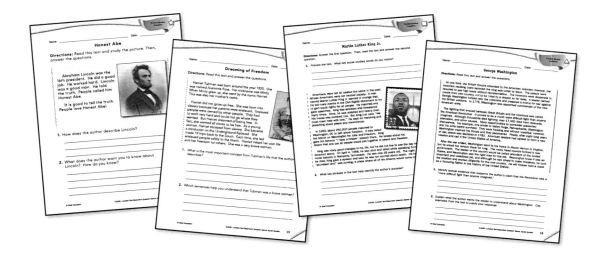

Implementing the Question Stems

This section includes 10 leveled, text-dependent question stems about understanding people, places, events, and concepts. You can implement these question stems by connecting them to the texts that you are reading in class.

It may seem as though using question stems would be easy, but it can be a complex task for teachers. To help you see how to implement these question stems in your classroom, this section includes student pages containing texts with sample text-dependent questions. Each of the four student pages illustrates a different complexity level.

Snapshot of Differentiating a Question

The chart below models how a single leveled question stem can be tied to social studies texts at four complexity levels. This snapshot also gives a quick view of how the question stems differ based on the complexity levels. However, you can also see how the question stems link to one another.

	Question Stem	Example
☆	What words or images tell about _____ (*person/place/event/concept*)?	What words or images tell about rules in school?
○	What is the main idea of page/section _____? How does this help you understand _____ (*person/place/event/concept*)?	What is the main idea of page 5? How does this help you understand the American flag?
☐	Identify the main idea of page/section _____. How does the main idea of this page/section help you understand _____ (*person/place/event/concept*)?	Identify the main idea of page 14. How does the main idea of this page help you understand the American Revolution?
△	Identify the main idea of page/section/chapter _____. How does this information contribute to your understanding of _____ (*person/place/event/concept*)?	Identify the main idea of section 2. How does this information contribute to your understanding of Southern leadership during the Civil War?

Understanding People, Places, Events, and Concepts Question Stems

Use these question stems to develop your own questions for students.

Preview the sentence/page. What does _____ (*word*) mean? What images do you see?

What words or images tell about _____ (*topic*)?

What is the main idea of the text? Where do you find it?

What words or images tell about _____ (*person/place/event/ concept*)?

How does the author describe _____ (*person/place/event/ concept*)?

What details can you find about _____ (*person/place/event/ concept*)?

What is the author's purpose? Which sentence tells you this?

What does the author want you to know about _____ (*person/ place/event/concept*)? How do you know?

Why does the author tell about _____ (*person/place/event/ concept*)?

What words or phrases help you understand _____ (*person/ place/event/concept*)?

Name: _____   Date: _____

Honest Abe

Directions: Read this text, and study the picture. Then, answer the questions.

Abraham Lincoln was the 16th president. He did a good job. He worked hard. Lincoln was a good man. He told the truth. People called him Honest Abe.

It is good to tell the truth. People love Honest Abe!

1. How does the author describe Lincoln?

_____

_____

_____

2. What does the author want you to know about Lincoln? How do you know?

_____

_____

_____

_____

Understanding People, Places, Events, and Concepts Question Stems

Use these question stems to develop your own questions for students.

Preview the paragraph/page. What social studies words and/or images do you see?

How are _____ (*word/image*) and _____ (*word/image*) connected to each other?

What is the main idea of the text? Where is it stated in the text?

What is the main idea of page/section _____? How does this help you understand _____ (*person/place/event/concept*)?

What/who is the most important person/place/event/concept that the author describes?

What details about _____ (*person/place/event/concept*) are included in the text?

What evidence is there that the author's purpose is to _____ (*persuade/inform/entertain*)?

What does the author want you to understand about _____ (*person/place/event/concept*)? Use details from the text to explain your answer.

What reasons does the author give for his/her claim or position?

Which words/phrases/sentences help you understand _____ (*person/place/event/concept*)?

Name: _____ Date: _____

Dreaming of Freedom

Directions: Read this text, and answer the questions.

Harriet Tubman was born around 1820. She was named Araminta Ross. Her nickname was Minty. When Minty grew up, she went by the name Harriet. This was also her mother's name.

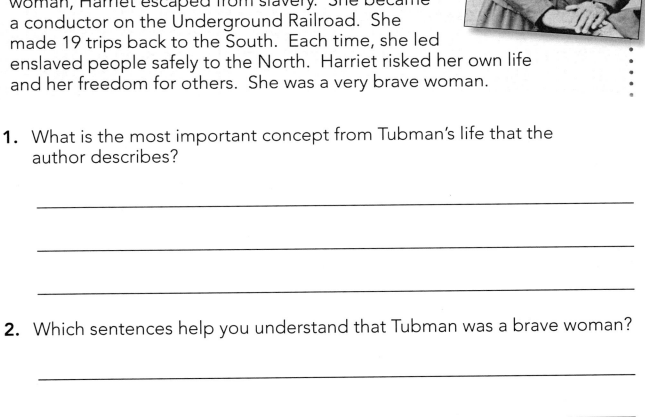

Harriet did not grow up free. She was born into slavery because her parents were enslaved. Enslaved people were owned by other people. They had to work very hard and could not go where they wanted. But Harriet dreamed of being free. In fact, she wanted all enslaved people to be free. As a young woman, Harriet escaped from slavery. She became a conductor on the Underground Railroad. She made 19 trips back to the South. Each time, she led enslaved people safely to the North. Harriet risked her own life and her freedom for others. She was a very brave woman.

1. What is the most important concept from Tubman's life that the author describes?

   _____

   _____

   _____

2. Which sentences help you understand that Tubman was a brave woman?

   _____

   _____

   _____

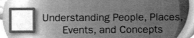

Understanding People, Places, Events, and Concepts Question Stems

Use these question stems to develop your own questions for students.

Preview the paragraph/text. What key social studies words and/ or images do you notice?

How do key social studies words and images relate to one another?

Identify the main idea of the text. Use textual evidence to support your answer.

Identify the main idea of page/section _____. How does the main idea of this page/section help you understand _____ (*person/place/event/concept*)?

Describe how the people/places/events/concepts on page _____ relate to the main idea.

What details about _____ (*person/place/event/concept*) does the author include in the text? Why do you think these details are important?

What key phrases/sentences in the text help identify the author's purpose?

What does the author want you to understand about _____ (*person/place/event/concept*)? Use evidence from the text to justify your answer.

Provide examples from the text to support the author's claim or position.

How does this text help you better understand _____ (*person/place/event/concept*)? Use evidence from the text to support your answer.

Name: _____ Date: _____

Martin Luther King Jr.

Directions: Answer the first question. Then, read the text, and answer the second question.

1.   Preview the text. What key social studies words and images do you notice?

_____

_____

_____

Americans were not all treated the same in the past. African Americans were not treated equally. A man named Martin Luther King Jr. wanted to change that. He led many events in the civil rights movement to try to gain equal rights for all people. He marched and gave speeches. King was arrested and threatened many times. Once, he was stabbed and nearly died. His house was bombed, too. But King just said, "We must meet hate with love." He kept on marching and preaching about peace and nonviolence.

In 1963, about 250,000 people marched to Washington, D.C., to talk about freedom. It was called the March on Washington for Jobs and Freedom. King gave his famous "I Have a Dream" speech there. He talked about his dream that one day all people would join together in peace and freedom.

King saw many good changes in his life, but he did not live to see the day he dreamed about. On April 4, 1968, he was shot and killed while speaking from his motel balcony in Memphis, Tennessee. He was only 39 years old. The night before he died, King gave a speech and said he was not worried about death. He knew the "promised land" was coming, a place where all of his dreams would come true.

2.   What key phrases in the text help identify the author's purpose?

_____

_____

_____

COMPLEXITY

LOW ★ ● ■ △ HIGH

Understanding People, Places, Events, and Concepts Question Stems

Use these question stems to develop your own questions for students.

Preview the text. Describe the important social studies words and/or images you notice.

Explain how the key social studies words and/or images relate to one another.

Identify the main idea of the text. Justify your answer with textual evidence.

Identify the main idea of page/section/chapter _____. How does this information contribute to your understanding of _____ (*person/place/event/concept*)?

Evaluate how the author relates _____ (*person/place/event/ concept*) to the main idea of the text.

Identify details about _____ (*person/place/event/concept*) that the author included in the text. Explain why these details are important and how they contribute to your understanding of the main idea.

Explain how key phrases/sentences on page _____ help you understand the author's purpose.

Explain what the author wants the reader to understand about _____ (*person/place/event/concept*). Cite examples from the text to justify your response.

Identify textual evidence that supports the author's claim or position.

Describe how this text helps you better understand _____ (*person/place/event/concept*). Use evidence from the text to support your response.

Name: _____   Date: _____

George Washington

Directions: Read this text, and answer the questions.

At one time, the British Empire extended to the American colonies; however, the colonists residing there believed the king was unfair to them. The people were required to pay high taxes without representation. The colonists were desperate to create their own country, not to be ruled by a despot so far away. A leader named George Washington helped rally the colonists and prepared a militia for war against the British soldiers. In 1775, Washington was appointed commander of the new American army.

The fighting that ensued between Great Britain and the colonists was called the American Revolution. It proved to be a much more difficult fight than anyone imagined. Although thousands died fighting, over 17,000 died from diseases, starvation, and other causes. Many opportunities to surrender presented themselves. For example, one winter in Valley Forge, Pennsylvania, Washington and his army barely survived. They were freezing and without supplies; however, Washington inspired his troops and they persevered. Finally, after eight long years of war, peace was declared in 1783. American leaders had agreed to form a new country and call it the United States of America.

After the war ended, Washington went to his home in Mount Vernon in Virginia, but he would not remain there for long. The newly freed country formed a new government. The leader of the country would be called president of the United States, and Washington was the right man for the job. Washington knew it was an important and undefined job, and although he was afraid to make mistakes, he took the position and worked diligently for the new country. He will forever hold a place as a Founding Father in the history of the United States.

1. Identify textual evidence that supports the author's claim that the Revolution was a "more difficult fight than anyone imagined."

_____

_____

_____

2. Explain what the author wants the reader to understand about Washington. Cite examples from the text to justify your response.

_____

_____

_____

Understanding People, Places, Events, and Concepts K–12 Alignment

Use this chart to determine the best question stems for your different groups of students.

★	●	■	▲
Preview the sentence/ page. What does _____ (word) mean? What images do you see?	Preview the paragraph/page. What social studies words and/or images do you see?	Preview the paragraph/text. What key social studies words and/or images do you notice?	Preview the text. Describe the important social studies words and/or images you notice.
What words or images tell about _____ (topic)?	How are _____ (word/image) and _____ (word/image) connected to each other?	How do key social studies words and images relate to one another?	Explain how the key social studies words and/or images relate to one another.
What is the main idea of the text? Where do you find it?	What is the main idea of the text? Where is it stated in the text?	Identify the main idea of the text. Use textual evidence to support your answer.	Identify the main idea of the text. Justify your answer with textual evidence.
What words or images tell about _____ (person/place/event/ concept)?	What is the main idea of page/section _____? How does this help you understand _____ (person/place/event/ concept)?	Identify the main idea of page/section _____. How does the main idea of this page/section help you understand _____ (person/place/event/ concept)?	Identify the main idea of page/section/ chapter _____. How does this information contribute to your understanding of _____ (person/ place/event/concept)?
How does the author describe _____ (person/place/event/ concept)?	What/who is the most important person/ place/event/concept that the author describes?	Describe how the people/places/ events/concepts on page _____ relate to the main idea.	Evaluate how the author relates _____ (person/place/event/ concept) to the main idea of the text.

Understanding People, Places, Events, and Concepts K–12 Alignment *(cont.)*

★	●	■	▲
What details can you find about _____ (person/place/event/concept)?	What details about _____ (person/place/event/concept) are included in the text?	What details about _____ (person/place/event/concept) does the author include in the text? Why do you think these details are important?	Identify details about _____ (person/place/event/concept) that the author included in the text. Explain why these details are important and how they contribute to your understanding of the main idea.
What is the author's purpose? Which sentence tells you this?	What evidence is there that the author's purpose is to _____ (persuade/inform/entertain)?	What key phrases/sentences in the text help identify the author's purpose?	Explain how key phrases/sentences on page _____ help you understand the author's purpose.
What does the author want you to know about _____ (person/place/event/concept)? How do you know?	What does the author want you to understand about _____ (person/place/event/concept)? Use details from the text to explain your answer.	What does the author want you to understand about _____ (person/place/event/concept)? Use evidence from the text to justify your answer.	Explain what the author wants the reader to understand about _____ (person/place/event/concept). Cite examples from the text to justify your response.
Why does the author tell about _____ (person/place/event/concept)?	What reasons does the author give for his/her claim or position?	Provide examples from the text to support the author's claim or position.	Identify textual evidence that supports the author's claim or position.
What words or phrases help you understand _____ (person/place/event/concept)?	Which words/phrases/sentences help you understand _____ (person/place/event/concept)?	How does this text help you better understand _____ (person/place/event/concept)? Use evidence from the text to support your answer.	Describe how this text helps you better understand _____ (person/place/event/concept). Use evidence from the text to support your response.

Identifying Key Details and Facts

Skill Overview

Identifying key details and facts in a text is an important step toward helping students understand how to use evidence from texts. Students must be able to identify relevant and significant details and explain how they support a main point or an author's claim or position. Students should be able to categorize several types of evidence, including facts, descriptions, and quotations. They should also be able to distinguish between fact and opinion. Helping students distinguish between types of evidence strengthens their abilities to explain how specific details are used to advance a position or an argument. Students should also be able to identify the steps in a process or a series of events and explain the significance of their order. These skills help students become discerning readers who can quickly identify the important pieces of a text.

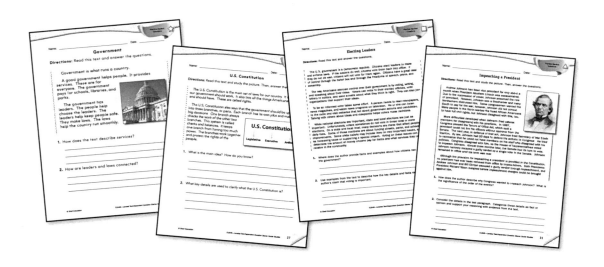

Implementing the Question Stems

This section includes 10 leveled, text-dependent question stems about identifying key details and facts. You can implement these question stems by connecting them to the texts that you are reading in class.

It may seem as though using question stems would be easy, but it can be a complex task for teachers. To help you see how to implement these question stems in your classroom, this section includes student pages containing texts with sample text-dependent questions. Each of the four student pages illustrates a different complexity level.

Snapshot of Differentiating a Question

The chart below models how a single leveled question stem can be tied to social studies texts at four complexity levels. This snapshot also gives a quick view of how the question stems differ based on the complexity levels. However, you can also see how the question stems link to one another.

	Question Stem	Example
☆	How does the text describe _____ (key detail/fact)?	How does the text describe the flag?
○	How does _____ (key detail/fact) support the author's claim or position?	How does the fact that George Washington was respected support the author's claim that he was a good president?
□	Use examples from the text to describe how the key details and facts support the author's claim or position.	Use examples from the text to describe how the key details and facts support the author's position that the Romans had a complex society.
△	In what ways do the key details support the author's claim or position? Use examples from the text to justify your reasoning.	In what ways do the key details support the author's position that the story of Pocahontas is mainly a legend? Use examples from the text to justify your reasoning.

Identifying Key Details and Facts
Question Stems

Use these question stems to develop your own questions for students.

What words tell about _____ (*main idea*)?

What are the important details?

Which words tell facts about _____ (*detail*)?

How are _____ (*detail/fact*) and _____ (*detail/fact*) connected?

How does the text describe _____ (*key detail/fact*)?

What examples show _____ (*author's claim or position*)?

Why is _____ (*relevant detail*) important?

Why does the author include _____ (*clarifying point to a key idea*)?

What is the _____ (*first/second/last*) step to _____ (*process/event*)?

Is _____ (*detail*) a fact or an opinion? How do you know?

Name: _____ Date: _____

Government

Directions: Read this text, and answer the questions.

Government is what runs a country.

A good government helps people. It provides services. These are for everyone. The government pays for schools, libraries, and parks.

The government has leaders. The people help choose the leaders. The leaders help keep people safe. They make laws. The laws help the country run smoothly.

1. How does the text describe *services*?

_____

_____

_____

2. How are leaders and laws connected?

_____

_____

_____

_____

COMPLEXITY

LOW  HIGH

Identifying Key Details and Facts Question Stems

Use these question stems to develop your own questions for students.

What is the main idea? How do you know?

What details support the main idea?

How do the facts/examples/descriptions/quotations relate to the key details?

Why does the author put the key details and facts in this order?

How does _____ (*key detail/fact*) support the author's claim or position?

The author claims _____ (*author's claim or position*). What details support this?

Is _____ (*relevant or irrelevant detail*) important to the main idea? Why or why not?

What key details or facts are used to clarify _____ (*key idea*)?

What are the steps to _____ (*process/event*)?

The text says _____ (*detail/quotation*). Is this a fact or an opinion? How do you know?

Name: _____ Date: _____

U.S. Constitution

Directions: Read this text, and study the diagram. Then, answer the questions.

The U.S. Constitution is the main set of laws for the country. It says how the U.S. government should work. It also lists all the things Americans can do and should have. These are called rights.

The U.S. Constitution also says that the government should be split into three branches, or parts. Each branch has its own jobs and makes big decisions. One branch always checks the work of the other two branches. This system is called checks and balances. It keeps one branch from having too much power. The branches work together and protect the rights of the people.

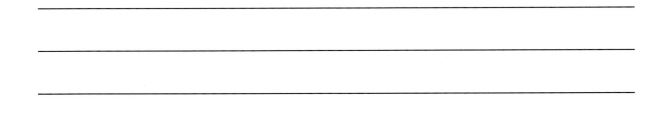

U.S. Constitution

Legislative   Executive   Judicial

1. What is the main idea? How do you know?

_____

_____

_____

2. What key details are used to clarify what the U.S. Constitution is?

_____

_____

_____

_____

COMPLEXITY

LOW ★ ● □ ▲ HIGH

Identifying Key Details and Facts Question Stems

Use these question stems to develop your own questions for students.

Identify the main idea of the text. Use evidence from the text to justify your answer.

What specific details from the text support the main idea?

Where does the author provide facts/examples/descriptions/ quotations about _____ (detail)?

Why does the author structure the key details and facts in this way?

Use examples from the text to describe how the key details and facts support the author's claim or position.

Which details or examples best support _____ (author's claim or position)?

Does _____ (relevant or irrelevant detail) support the author's claim? Why or why not? Why did the author include it?

Describe any key details or facts the author uses to clarify a point or key idea.

Describe the details from the text that outline the steps to _____ (process/event).

Review the details of the paragraphs/sentences on page _____. Which details are facts, and which are the author's opinion?

Name: _____ Date: _____

Electing Leaders

Directions: Read this text, and answer the questions.

The U.S. government is a democratic republic. Citizens elect leaders to make and enforce laws. If the leaders do well, citizens vote them back into office. If they do not do well, citizens may not vote for them again. Citizens have a great deal of control through the ballot box and through the freedoms of speech, press, and assembly.

The way Americans exercise control over their government is by voting, writing, and speaking about their views. Voters can write to their elected officials, write letters to editors, and send e-mails about what they think is right. They can also join organizations that support their ideas.

To be an informed voter takes some effort. A person needs to read newspapers and news magazines and watch news programs on television. He or she can listen to the radio and visit websites that discuss government actions and candidates. Talking with others about ideas and viewpoints helps voters make decisions.

While national elections are important, state and local elections are just as important. Unfortunately, voters sometimes do not vote in those local or state elections. On a state and local level, many decisions are made that affect people's daily lives. Some of those elections are about funding streets, parks, and school improvements. Some state ballots may include laws on very important issues, such as increasing taxes or supporting a special project. Voting on these issues can determine the amount of money citizens pay for items and what services they can receive in the community.

1. Where does the author provide facts and examples about how citizens can affect the government?

   _____

   _____

2. Use examples from the text to describe how the key details and facts support the author's claim that voting is important.

   _____

   _____

   _____

Identifying Key Details and Facts
Question Stems

Use these question stems to develop your own questions for students.

Identify the main idea of the text. Cite specific evidence from the text to justify your response.

Describe how the author uses specific details to support the main idea.

Read the paragraph/text and categorize the types of evidence (*facts/examples/descriptions/quotations*) the author includes.

How do the key details and facts in each paragraph build upon each other to develop the central claim or position?

In what ways do the key details support the author's claim or position? Use examples from the text to justify your reasoning.

Identify the most important details from the text, and describe how they support _____ (*author's claim or position*).

The author includes _____ (*relevant or irrelevant detail*). Does this detail support the author's claim or position? Why does the author include it?

Explain how the author clarifies points and key ideas in the text.

How does the author describe _____ (*process/event*)? What is the significance of the order of the steps/events?

Consider the details of the paragraphs/sentences on page _____. Categorize these details as fact or opinion, and support your reasoning with evidence from the text.

Name: _____ Date: _____

Impeaching a President

Directions: Read this text, and study the picture. Then, answer the questions.

Andrew Johnson had been vice president for only about a month when President Abraham Lincoln was assassinated. Through the succession of power, Johnson assumed the role of president. However, Johnson was a Southerner, and many Northerners distrusted him. Some congressmen wanted the South to pay for the war; however, Johnson did not concur. Many people in the North wanted the freed African Americans to have full civil rights, but Johnson disagreed with this, too.

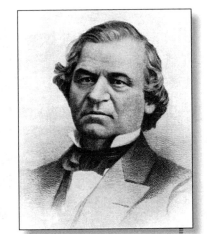

More difficulties developed when Johnson fired cabinet members for disagreeing with his positions. In 1867, Congress passed the Tenure of Office Act, which said a president could not fire his officers without approval from the Senate. The next year, in defiance of that act, Johnson fired Secretary of War Edwin Stanton. By law, Johnson had 20 days to defend his actions to Congress. He tried to rationalize that he could not have members on his staff who disagreed with his policies. Congress did not accept this explanation, so the House of Representatives voted to impeach Johnson. Almost three months later, the Senate had its turn to vote. Johnson narrowly escaped a guilty verdict by a single vote in the Senate. Johnson remained in office until his term was over.

Although the provision for impeaching a president is provided in the Constitution, no president has ever been removed from office by impeachment. Both Presidents Andrew Johnson and Bill Clinton escaped removal from office because they failed to receive a majority vote from the Senate. President Richard Nixon was never removed from office because he resigned before impeachment charges could be brought against him.

1. How does the author describe why Congress wanted to impeach Johnson? What is the significance of the order of the events?

   _____

   _____

2. Consider the details in the last paragraph. Categorize these details as fact or opinion, and support your reasoning with evidence from the text.

   _____

   _____

Identifying Key Details and Facts
K–12 Alignment

Use this chart to determine the best question stems for your different groups of students.

★	●	■	▲
What words tell about _____ (*main idea*)?	What is the main idea? How do you know?	Identify the main idea of the text. Use evidence from the text to justify your answer.	Identify the main idea of the text. Cite specific evidence from the text to justify your response.
What are the important details?	What details support the main idea?	What specific details from the text support the main idea?	Describe how the author uses specific details to support the main idea.
Which words tell facts about _____ (*detail*)?	How do the facts/examples/ descriptions/ quotations relate to the key details?	Where does the author provide facts/examples/ descriptions/ quotations about _____ (*detail*)?	Read the paragraph/text and categorize the types of evidence (*facts/examples/ descriptions/quotations*) the author includes.
How are _____ (*detail/fact*) and _____ (*detail/fact*) connected?	Why does the author put the key details and facts in this order?	Why does the author structure the key details and facts in this way?	How do the key details and facts in each paragraph build upon each other to develop the central claim or position?
How does the text describe _____ (*key detail/fact*)?	How does _____ (*key detail/fact*) support the author's claim or position?	Use examples from the text to describe how the key details and facts support the author's claim or position.	In what ways do the key details support the author's claim or position? Use examples from the text to justify your reasoning.

Identifying Key Details and Facts
K–12 Alignment *(cont.)*

★	●	■	▲
What examples show _____ (*author's claim or position*)?	The author claims _____ (*author's claim or position*). What details support this?	Which details or examples best support _____ (*author's claim or position*)?	Identify the most important details from the text, and describe how they support _____ (*author's claim or position*).
Why is _____ (*relevant detail*) important?	Is _____ (*relevant or irrelevant detail*) important to the main idea? Why or why not?	Does _____ (*relevant or irrelevant detail*) support the author's claim? Why or why not? Why did the author include it?	The author includes _____ (*relevant or irrelevant detail*). Does this detail support the author's claim or position? Why does the author include it?
Why does the author include _____ (*clarifying point to a key idea*)?	What key details or facts are used to clarify _____ (*key idea*)?	Describe any key details or facts the author uses to clarify a point or key idea.	Explain how the author clarifies points and key details in the text.
What is the _____ (*first/second/last*) step to _____ (*process/event*)?	What are the steps to _____ (*process/event*)?	Describe the details from the text that outline the steps to _____ (*process/event*).	How does the author describe _____ (*process/event*)? What is the significance of the order of the steps/events?
Is _____ (*detail*) a fact or an opinion? How do you know?	The text says _____ (*detail/quotation*). Is this a fact or an opinion? How do you know?	Review the details of the paragraphs/sentences on page _____. Which details are facts, and which are the author's opinion?	Consider the details of the paragraphs/sentences on page _____. Categorize these details as fact or opinion, and support your reasoning with evidence from the text.

Summarizing Positions

Skill Overview

Summarization is an effective way to improve comprehension. The ability to summarize positions provides the foundation for students to conduct higher-level analysis, such as evaluating arguments. To summarize positions, students must first be able to identify positions and conclusions drawn in the text. Then, they must explain the key ideas of those positions and conclusions using the most relevant information from the text.

Students must evaluate and judge which key ideas and details are most important and which can be left out of a summary. Students must also be able to justify their responses with evidence from the text, including what the author chooses to focus on and what the author provides the most details and information about in the text. Students should be able to summarize text in a variety of ways, such as verbally, through writing, and by creating time lines or flow maps of the events in a text.

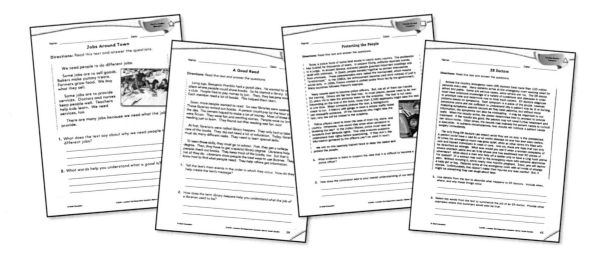

Implementing the Question Stems

This section includes 10 leveled, text-dependent question stems about summarizing positions. You can implement these question stems by connecting them to texts that you are reading in class.

It may seem as though using question stems would be easy, but it can be a complex task for teachers. To help you see how to implement these question stems in your classroom, this section includes student pages containing texts with sample text-dependent questions. Each of the four student pages illustrates a different complexity level.

Snapshot of Differentiating a Question

The chart below models how a single leveled question stem can be tied to social studies texts at four complexity levels. This snapshot also gives a quick view of how the question stems differ based on the complexity levels. However, you can also see how the question stems link to one another.

	Question Stem	Example
☆	What happened to _____ (*person/group*)?	What happened to the American Indians?
○	What happened to _____ (*person/group*) and why?	What happened to the immigrants and why?
▢	What happened to _____ (*person/group*)? When, where, and why did this happen?	What happened to enslaved people? When, where, and why did this happen?
△	Use details from the text to describe what happened to _____ (*person/group*). Include when, where, and why this occurred.	Use details from the text to describe what happened to Jewish people in Germany. Include when, where, and why this occurred.

Summarizing Positions Question Stems

Use these question stems to develop your own questions for students.

What happened to _____ (*person/group*)?

What words help you understand _____ (*concept*)?

What does the text say about _____ (*concept*)?

What happens at the end of the text?

How does _____ (*concept*) connect to _____ (*conclusion*)?

What does the text say about _____ (*conclusion*)?

How can you connect _____ (*conclusion*) to you?

Tell the text's events in the order in which they happen.

Which sentence(s) or phrase(s) do you think is/are the most important?

What is one important idea from the text?

Name: _____ Date: _____

Jobs Around Town

Directions: Read this text, and answer the questions.

We need people to do different jobs.

Some jobs are to sell goods. Bakers make yummy treats. Farmers grow food. We buy what they sell.

Some jobs are to provide services. Doctors and nurses keep people well. Teachers help kids learn. We need services, too.

There are many jobs because we need what the jobs provide.

1. What does the text say about why we need people to do different jobs?

   _____

   _____

   _____

2. What words help you understand what a *good* is?

   _____

   _____

   _____

Summarizing Positions Question Stems

Use these question stems to develop your own questions for students.

What happened to _____ (*person/group*) and why?

How do the words _____ and _____ help you understand _____ (*concept*)?

Find details in the text to tell about _____ (*concept*).

What is the conclusion of the text?

What central concepts or ideas support _____ (*conclusion*)?

How does _____ (*conclusion*) help you understand _____ (*person/place/event/time period/concept*)?

How does _____ (*conclusion*) help you understand our world?

Tell the text's events in the order in which they occur. How do they help create the text's message?

What quotations support the most important ideas in the text?

Which is the most important idea in the text?

Name: _____   Date: _____

A Good Read

Directions: Read this text, and answer the questions.

Long ago, Benjamin Franklin had a good idea. He wanted to open a place where people could share books. So he started a library. It was like a club. People had to pay money to join. Then, they became members. Each member read a lot of books. This helped them learn.

Soon, more people wanted to read. So new libraries were opened. These libraries rented out books. A person could pay by the hour or by the day. The owners hoped to make a lot of money. Most of these books were fiction. They were fun and exciting stories. People were no longer reading just to learn. They found out that reading was fun, too!

At first, librarians were called *library keepers*. They only had to take care of the books. They did not need a lot of education. Today, librarians must do many different tasks. They need to learn special skills.

To learn these skills, they must go to school. First, they get a college degree. Then, they have to get a special library degree. Librarians help people check out books. They keep track of the books, too. But that is not all they do. Librarians show people the best ways to use libraries. They know how to find what people need. They help others get information.

1. Tell the text's main events in the order in which they occur. How do they help create the text's message?

   _____

   _____

2. How does the term *library keepers* help you understand what the job of a librarian used to be?

   _____

   _____

Summarizing Positions Question Stems

Use these question stems to develop your own questions for students.

What happened to _____ (*person/group*)? When, where, and why did this happen?

Use key words from the text to summarize _____ (*concept*).

What evidence is there to support _____ (*concept*)?

What conclusions can be drawn at the end of the text?

How is _____ (*conclusion*) related to the central concept or idea of the text?

How does the conclusion add to your understanding of _____ (*person/place/event/time period/concept*)?

How does _____ (*conclusion*) add to your understanding of how our world and cultures around the world work?

Make a time line of events in the text. How do these events support the main points from page/section _____?

Create a flow map of quotations from the text that capture the most important ideas.

What conclusion or key idea can you draw from this text?

Name: _____ Date: _____

Protecting the People

Directions: Read this text, and answer the questions.

Today, a police force of some kind exists in nearly every country. The profession has existed for thousands of years. In ancient China, prefects reported crimes to a judge. In ancient Greece, enslaved people guarded important meetings and dealt with criminals. In Spain, people banded together to protect themselves from criminals. These peacekeepers were called the *Hermandad*, which means "brotherhood." In the 1660s, law enforcement became paid work instead of just a social duty. In 1666, France created a unified police force led by the government. Many countries followed France's example.

Many people want to become police officers. But, not all of them can handle the training. Others will fail the final test. In most places, people need to be over 21 years old to take the entrance exam for the academy. The test is not easy. Depending on the size of the force, more than 3,000 applicants might take the test at one time. When someone passes the test, a background check is run. A history with gangs or even a simple traffic ticket can disqualify someone. Of the thousands who might take the test, very few will be invited to the academy.

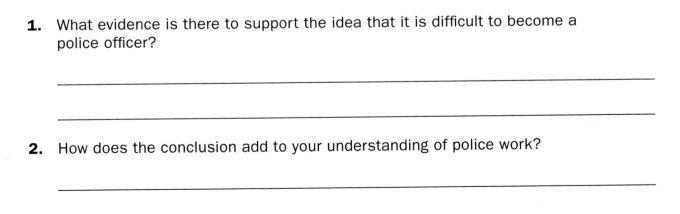

Police officers need to know the laws of their city, state, and country. Otherwise, how would they know when someone is breaking the law? In the United States, police must read all suspects their Miranda rights. This step ensures that suspects understand their rights before questioning. If they don't, the information gathered by the officers can't be used in court.

We rely on this specially trained force to keep the peace and protect the people.

1. What evidence is there to support the idea that it is difficult to become a police officer?

   _____

   _____

2. How does the conclusion add to your understanding of police work?

   _____

   _____

Summarizing Positions Question Stems

Use these question stems to develop your own questions for students.

Use details from the text to describe what happened to _____ (*person/group*). Include when, where, and why this occurred.

Use key words from the text to summarize _____ (*concept*). Provide other examples where this summary would also be true.

Is there evidence to support an idea that is not clearly stated? Cite specific examples from the text.

What important conclusion does the author make at the end of the text?

Summarize _____ (*conclusion*) and identify the central concepts or ideas that support this conclusion.

Describe how the conclusion increases your understanding of _____ (*person/place/event/time period/concept*).

In what ways does _____ (*conclusion*) increase your understanding of our world and cultures around the world?

Create a time line of events, and summarize how they help support the author's main points from page/section _____.

Identify the quotation that best supports the author's main points. Describe how and why it is the best quotation.

Summarize the conclusions or key ideas that you can draw from the text, and explain how they are supported in the text.

Name: _____ Date: _____

ER Doctors

Directions: Read this text, and answer the questions.

Across the country, emergency room (ER) doctors treat more than 100 million patients every year. Many patients arrive at the emergency room seeking relief for aches and pains. Some are serious cases, while others are not. The ER doctor must have extensive knowledge of a variety of conditions and diseases in order to prioritize care and determine how to treat each patient. ER doctors diagnose patients based on symptoms. Each symptom is a piece of the puzzle; however, symptoms alone are not sufficient to understand why a patient may be ill or hurting. Analyzing symptoms assists doctors as they treat patients, but without more information, the symptoms can also be misleading. It may be important to run tests. When the results arrive, the doctor determines how to provide treatment. If the results are good, the patient may not need further treatment and can return home. Other times, the results may indicate that the patient needs to consult a specialist. In extreme circumstances, test results will indicate that a patient needs surgery immediately.

The only thing ER doctors can expect while they are on duty is the unexpected. A patient could have a bad flu or an exotic disease no one has ever seen before. At times, the emergency room may grow quiet, while at other times it's filled with sick and injured individuals in need of care. And yet, there are days that can only be described as strange. What else would you call it when a woman complains of severe stomach pains and an X-ray shows she has swallowed over 50 pieces of silverware? What about a man who falls off a ladder only to have a long hook pierce his eyeball? Or a woman may rush to the emergency room with extreme abdominal pain. Without knowing it, she's nearly nine months pregnant. Soon, she will deliver a baby girl or boy. Patients arrive at the emergency room with all kinds of strange stories. Unfortunately, that doesn't make their injuries any less painful! But it might be something they can laugh about later.

1. Use details from the text to describe what happens to ER doctors. Include when, where, and why these things occur.

_____

_____

2. Use key words from the text to summarize the job of an ER doctor. Provide other examples where this summary would also be true.

_____

_____

Summarizing Positions K–12 Alignment

Use this chart to determine the best question stems for your different groups of students.

★	●	■	▲
What happened to _____ (person/group)?	What happened to _____ (person/group) and why?	What happened to _____ (person/group)? When, where, and why did this happen?	Use details from the text to describe what happened to _____ (person/group). Include when, where, and why this occurred.
What words help you understand _____ (concept)?	How do the words _____ and _____ help you understand _____ (concept)?	Use key words from the text to summarize _____ (concept).	Use key words from the text to summarize _____ (concept). Provide other examples where this summary would also be true.
What does the text say about _____ (concept)?	Find details in the text to tell about _____ (concept).	What evidence is there to support _____ (concept)?	Is there evidence to support an idea that is not clearly stated? Cite specific examples from the text.
What happens at the end of the text?	What is the conclusion of the text?	What conclusions can be drawn at the end of the text?	What important conclusion does the author make at the end of the text?
How does _____ (concept) connect to _____ (conclusion)?	What central concepts or ideas support _____ (conclusion)?	How is _____ (conclusion) related to the central concept or idea of the text?	Summarize _____ (conclusion) and identify the central concepts or ideas that support this conclusion.

Summarizing Positions K–12 Alignment *(cont.)*

★	●	■	▲
What does the text say about _____ (conclusion)?	How does _____ (conclusion) help you understand _____ (person/place/event/time period/concept)?	How does the conclusion add to your overall understanding of _____ (person/place/event/time period/concept)?	Describe how the conclusion increases your understanding of _____ (person/place/event/time period/concept).
How can you connect _____ (conclusion) to you?	How does _____ (conclusion) help you understand our world?	How does _____ (conclusion) add to your understanding of how our world and cultures around the world work?	In what ways does _____ (conclusion) increase your understanding of our world and cultures around the world?
Tell the text's events in the order in which they happen.	Tell the text's events in the order in which they occur. How do they help create the text's message?	Make a time line of events in the text. How do these events support the main points from page/section _____?	Create a time line of events, and summarize how they help support the author's main points from page/section _____.
Which sentence(s) or phrase(s) do you think is/are the most important?	What quotations support the most important ideas in the text?	Create a flow map of quotations from the text that capture the most important ideas.	Identify the quotation that best supports the author's main points. Describe how and why it is the best quotation.
What is one important idea from the text?	What is the most important idea in the text?	What conclusion or key idea can you draw from this text?	Summarize the conclusions or key ideas that you can draw from the text, and explain how they are supported in the text.

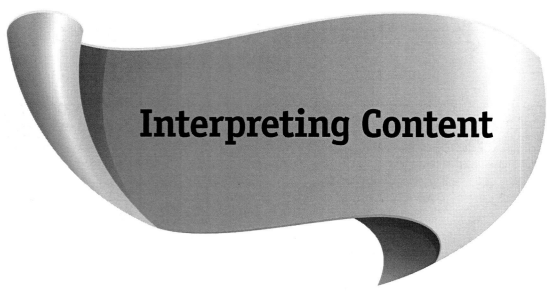

Interpreting Content

Skill Overview

Interpreting content helps students unlock the meaning behind a text. This skill requires students to transform their understandings of the text using words or images, as appropriate for the task and grade level. Interpreting content includes the abilities to paraphrase and summarize. It also provides students the opportunity to use evidence from a text to clarify their understandings of the text. Students analyze the meaning of a text as a whole, in sections, and in individual quotes. They explain how their understandings of these parts contribute to their understandings of the topic of study. They also learn to visualize the meaning of the text and communicate that meaning in a variety of ways. The application of this skill helps deepen comprehension as students use their background knowledge to expand upon their understandings of the text.

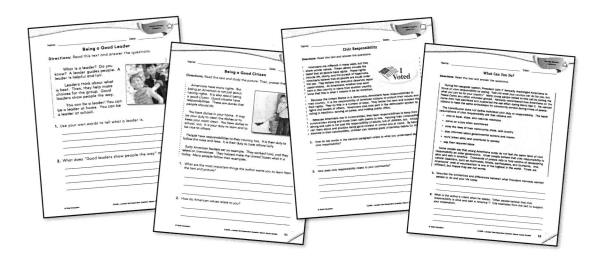

Implementing the Question Stems

This section includes 10 leveled, text-dependent question stems about interpreting content. You can implement these question stems by connecting them to the texts that you are reading in class.

It may seem as though using question stems would be easy, but it can be a complex task for teachers. To help you see how to implement these question stems in your classroom, this section includes student pages containing texts with sample text-dependent questions. Each of the four student pages illustrates a different complexity level.

Snapshot of Differentiating a Question

The chart below models how a single leveled question stem can be tied to social studies texts at four complexity levels. This snapshot also gives a quick view of how the question stems differ based on the complexity levels. However, you can also see how the question stems link to one another.

	Question Stem	Example
☆	What about _____ (*event/time period/concept*) is the same as your life?	What about people long ago is the same as your life?
◯	What is different about _____ (*event/time period/concept*) and your life? Describe how it is different.	What is different about the 1700s and your life? Describe how it is different.
▢	How is _____ (*event/time period/concept*) similar to and different from your life today?	How is life in ancient Greece similar to and different from your life today?
△	Describe the similarities and differences between _____ (*event/time period/concept*) and your life today.	Describe the similarities and differences between the Gilded Age and your life today.

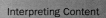

COMPLEXITY

Interpreting Content Question Stems

Use these question stems to develop your own questions for students.

How does the word _____ help you understand _____ (*person/place/event/time period/concept*)?

What does _____ (*person/place/event/time period/concept*) have to do with you?

What about _____ (*event/time period/concept*) is the same as your life?

Use your own words to tell about _____ (*paragraph/text*).

What does _____ (*quotation*) mean?

Draw a picture to show what the text is about.

Draw a picture to show what the author means when he/she states, _____ (*quotation*).

The text describes _____ (*concept*). What else does this remind you of?

What is one important thing to learn from this text?

What is the text mainly about? What part of the text tells you this?

Name: _____ Date: _____

Being a Good Leader

Directions: Read this text, and answer the questions.

What is a leader? Do you know? A leader guides people. A leader is helpful and fair.

Leaders think about what is best. Then, they help make choices for the group. Good leaders show people the way.

You can be a leader! You can be a leader at home. You can be a leader at school.

1. Use your own words to tell what a leader is.

_____

_____

_____

_____

2. What does "Good leaders show people the way" mean?

_____

_____

_____

_____

Interpreting Content Question Stems

Use these question stems to develop your own questions for students.

What key words help you understand _____ (*person/place/ event/time period/concept*)?

How does _____ (*person/place/event/time period/concept*) relate to you?

What is different about _____ (*event/time period/concept*) and your life? Describe how it is different.

Rewrite _____ (*paragraph/text*) in your own words.

What does the author mean when he/she states, _____ (*quotation*)?

What images would best explain what the author is describing?

The text uses the words _____ (*quotation*) to describe _____ (*person/place/event/time period/concept*). How do these words help you picture what the author is saying?

What is another way to explain what the text says about _____ (*concept*)?

What are the most important things the author wants you to learn from this text?

What is the main point of the text? What details does the author give to help you understand it?

Name: _____ Date: _____

Being a Good Citizen

Directions: Read this text, and study the picture. Then, answer the questions.

Americans have many rights. But being an American is not just about having rights. It is also about being a good citizen. Good citizens have responsibilities. These are duties that people should do.

You have duties in your home. It may be your duty to clean the dishes or to keep your room clean. You have duties in school, too. It is your duty to learn and to be nice to others.

People have responsibilities to their country, too. It is their duty to follow the rules and laws. It is their duty to treat others fairly.

Early American leaders set an example. They worked hard, and they relied on themselves. They helped make the United States what it is today. Many people follow their examples.

1. What are the most important things the author wants you to learn from the text and picture?

   _____

   _____

   _____

2. How does being a good citizen relate to you?

   _____

   _____

Interpreting Content Question Stems

Use these question stems to develop your own questions for students.

How do key words in the text relate to what you understand about _____ (*person/place/event/time period/concept*)?

How does _____ (*person/place/event/time period/concept*) relate to your community?

How is _____ (*event/time period/concept*) similar to and different from your life today?

Use key content words to rewrite _____ (*paragraph/text*) in your own words.

What is the author trying to communicate when he/she states, _____ (*quotation*)? Use examples from the text to support your explanation.

What images would you use to explain what the author is trying to communicate? Why?

Visualize what the author is communicating about _____ (*person/place/event/time period/concept*) on page _____. Describe what you "see."

What analogy can be made for the concept the author is describing on page _____?

Summarize what the author is communicating in this text.

What is the main point of the text? What details does the author provide to help you understand it?

Name: _____ Date: _____

Civic Responsibility

Directions: Read this text, and answer the questions.

Americans are different in many ways, but they share similar values. These values include the belief that all people have rights. Those rights include life, liberty, and the pursuit of happiness. Americans believe that all people are equal under the law. They believe that everyone deserves equal opportunities. All Americans, whether they were born in this country or came from another country, know that this is what it means to be an American.

Because the United States is a democracy, Americans have responsibilities to their country. It is the responsibility of American citizens to protect their values and their rights. They do this in a number of ways. They follow the laws and respect the rights and beliefs of others. Americans also take part in the democratic system by voting in elections, serving on juries, and holding public office.

Because Americans live in communities, they have responsibilities to keep their communities strong and make them safe places to live. Keeping their communities strong and safe is not just the responsibility of adults, but of children, too. Children can learn about and practice being good citizens in school and at home. By being involved in their communities, children can develop good citizenship habits for life.

1. How do key words in the second paragraph relate to what you understand about civic responsibility?

   _____

   _____

   _____

2. How does civic responsibility relate to your community?

   _____

   _____

   _____

   _____

Interpreting Content Question Stems

Use these question stems to develop your own questions for students.

How do key words impact your understanding of _____ (*person/ place/event/time period/concept*)?

Explain how _____ (*person/place/event/time period/concept*) relates to your everyday life or your community.

Describe the similarities and differences between _____ (*event/time period/concept*) and your life today.

Summarize _____ (*paragraph/text*), including the key content words as needed.

What is the author's intent when he/she states, _____ (*quotation*)? Cite examples from the text to support your explanation.

What images would you use to explain what the author is trying to communicate? Justify your response with evidence from the text.

Visualize what the author is communicating about _____ (*person/place/event/time period/concept*) on page _____. Write a short paragraph describing what you understand.

Consider the concept the author is describing on page _____. Write an analogy that captures what the author is communicating.

Using only 200 words, explain what the author is communicating in this text.

Identify the main point of the text. Cite details the author provides to further explain the main point.

Name: _____ Date: _____

What Can You Do?

Directions: Read this text, and answer the questions.

During his inaugural speech, President John F. Kennedy challenged Americans to focus on civic responsibility by saying: "Ask not what your country can do for you, but what you can do for your country." Many young people rallied to this call by joining the Peace Corps and other volunteer groups. Kennedy remembered how Americans on the home front had sacrificed and supported the war effort during World War II. He wanted citizens to have the same enthusiasm for community service during times of peace.

The Constitution does not define individual civic duty or responsibility. The basic assumptions of civic responsibility are that citizens will:

- vote in local, state, and national elections

- serve on a jury when summoned

- obey the laws of their community, state, and country

- stay informed about governmental actions and issues

- work (when able) and contribute to society

- pay their required taxes

Some people say that young Americans today do not feel the same level of civic responsibility as older generations. Other people believe that civic responsibility is alive and well in America. Thousands of people rally to help victims of devastating natural disasters, such as hurricanes, floods, earthquakes, and tsunamis. And, Americans' level of volunteerism is one of the highest in the world. Times are different, but maybe they are not worse.

1. Describe the similarities and differences between what President Kennedy wanted people to do and your life today.

   _____

   _____

2. What is the author's intent when he states, "Other people believe that civic responsibility is alive and well in America"? Cite examples from the text to support your explanation.

   _____

   _____

   _____

Interpreting Content K–12 Alignment

Use this chart to determine the best question stems for your different groups of students.

★	●	■	▲
How does the word _____ help you understand _____ (*person/place/event/time period/concept*)?	What key words help you understand _____ (*person/place/event/time period/concept*)?	How do key words in the text relate to what you understand about _____ (*person/place/event/time period/concept*)?	How do key words impact your understanding of _____ (*person/place/event/time period/concept*)?
What does _____ (*person/place/event/time period/concept*) have to do with you?	How does _____ (*person/place/event/time period/concept*) relate to you?	How does _____ (*person/place/event/time period/concept*) relate to your community?	Explain how _____ (*person/place/event/time period/concept*) relates to your everyday life or your community.
What about _____ (*event/time period/concept*) is the same as your life?	What is different about _____ (*event/time period/concept*) and your life? Describe how it is different.	How is _____ (*event/time period/concept*) similar to and different from your life today?	Describe the similarities and differences between _____ (*event/time period/concept*) and your life today.
Use your own words to tell about _____ (*paragraph/text*).	Rewrite _____ (*paragraph/text*) in your own words.	Use key content words to rewrite _____ (*paragraph/text*) in your own words.	Summarize _____ (*paragraph/text*), including the key content words as needed.
What does _____ (*quotation*) mean?	What does the author mean when he/she states, _____ (*quotation*)?	What is the author trying to communicate when he/she states, _____ (*quotation*)? Use examples from the text to support your explanation.	What is the author's intent when he/she states, _____ (*quotation*)? Cite examples from the text to support your explanation.

Interpreting Content K–12 Alignment *(cont.)*

★	●	■	▲
Draw a picture to show what the text is about.	What images would best explain what the author is describing?	What images would you use to explain what the author is trying to communicate? Why?	What images would you use to explain what the author is trying to communicate? Justify your response with evidence from the text.
Draw a picture to show what the author means when he/she states, _____ (quotation).	The text uses the words _____ (quotation) to describe _____ (person/place/event/time period/concept). How do these words help you picture what the author is saying?	Visualize what the author is communicating about _____ (person/place/event/time period/concept) on page _____. Describe what you "see."	Visualize what the author is communicating about _____ (person/place/event/time period/concept) on page _____. Write a short paragraph describing what you understand.
The text describes _____ (concept). What else does this remind you of?	What is another way to explain what the text says about _____ (concept)?	What analogy can be made for the concept the author is describing on page _____?	Consider the concept the author is describing on page _____. Write an analogy that captures what the author is communicating.
What is one important thing to learn from this text?	What are the most important things the author wants you to learn from this text?	Summarize what the author is communicating in this text.	Using only 200 words, explain what the author is communicating in this text.
What is the text mainly about? What part of the text tells you this?	What is the main point of the text? What details does the author give to help you understand it?	What is the main point of the text? What details does the author provide to help you understand it?	Identify the main point of the text. Cite details the author provides to further explain the main point.

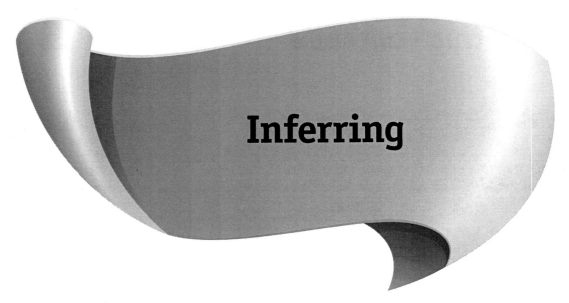

Inferring

Skill Overview

Students make inferences by combining their background knowledge with information from the text. Inferential information is not stated explicitly, but it can be reasonably assumed based on the information in the text. By inferring, students make predictions or hypotheses about people, places, events, or concepts. Inferring allows students to draw conclusions, pose alternative solutions, and consider how historical figures may react when faced with challenges or the reasons they reacted as they did. Students must have ample evidence in the text to support their inferences. They should be able to identify the portion of the text or the detail that supports an inference. Making inferences from the text increases students' capacities for critical thinking as they read between the lines of the text to understand implied meaning and consider potential outcomes of events.

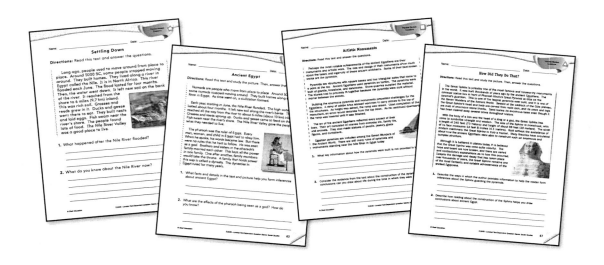

Implementing the Question Stems

This section includes 10 leveled, text-dependent question stems about inferring. You can implement these question stems by connecting them to the texts that you are reading in class.

It may seem as though using question stems would be easy, but it can be a complex task for teachers. To help you see how to implement these question stems in your classroom, this section includes student pages containing texts with sample text-dependent questions. Each of the four student pages illustrates a different complexity level.

Snapshot of Differentiating a Question

The chart below models how a single leveled question stem can be tied to social studies texts at four complexity levels. This snapshot also gives a quick view of how the question stems differ based on the complexity levels. However, you can also see how the question stems link to one another.

	Question Stem	Example
☆	What do you think would happen if _____ (event)?	What do you think would happen if Sacagawea were not able to go with Lewis and Clark?
○	Based on what you know about _____ (person/place/event/ time period/concept), what do you think would happen if _____ (event)?	Based on what you know about the United States before the Civil War, what do you think would happen if Harriet Tubman were caught?
☐	Based on what you understand about _____ (person/place/ event/time period/concept), predict what would happen if _____ (event).	Based on what you understand about the American Revolution, predict what would happen if the Americans were not able to raise an army.
△	Predict what would happen if _____ (event). How does your understanding about _____ (person/place/event/time period/concept) influence your prediction?	Predict what would happen if a group of people resisted Roman rule. How does your understanding about the Roman Empire influence your prediction?

Inferring Question Stems

Use these question stems to develop your own questions for students.

What do you know about _____ (*person/place/event/time period/concept*)?

What details or pictures in the text help you learn what happened?

What key information is missing from the text?

What do you think would happen if _____ (*event*)?

What would happen if _____ (*different outcome*)?

What will _____ (*person/group*) do?

What happened after _____ (*cause/s*)?

Think about what you read. If _____ (*event*) happened, then what might happen/be true?

What do you know about _____ (*person/place/event/concept*) now?

What was life like during _____ (*time period/event*)?

Name: _____ Date: _____

Settling Down

Directions: Read this text, and answer the questions.

Long ago, people used to move around from place to place. Around 5000 BC, some people stopped moving around. They built homes. They lived along a river in Egypt called the Nile. It is in North Africa. This river flooded each June. The flood lasted for four months. Then, the water went down. It left new soil on the bank of the river. It reached from the shore to 6 miles (9.7 km) inland. This was rich soil. Grasses and reeds grew in it. Ducks and geese went there to eat. They built nests and laid eggs. Fish swam near the river's shore. The people found a lot of food. The Nile River Valley was a good place to live.

1. What happened after the Nile River flooded?

_____

_____

_____

2. What do you know about the Nile River now?

_____

_____

_____

_____

Inferring Question Stems

Use these question stems to develop your own questions for students.

What do you already know about _____ (*person/place/event/ time period/concept*)?

What facts and details in the text help you form inferences about _____ (*person/place/event/time period/concept*)?

What key information is not provided in the text?

Based on what you know about _____ (*person/place/event/ time period/concept*), what do you think would happen if _____ (*event*)?

How would the outcome change if _____ (*event*) happened instead?

How will _____ (*person/group*) respond to _____ (*event*)?

What are the effects of _____ (*cause/s*)? How do you know?

Read paragraph/sentence _____ on page _____. Complete the following sentence: If..., then....

After reading about _____ (*time period/event*), what do you know about _____ (*person/place/event/concept*)?

Think about what you read about _____ (*concept*). What can you say about life during _____ (*time period/event*)?

Name: _____ Date: _____

Ancient Egypt

Directions: Read this text, and study the picture. Then, answer the questions.

Nomads are people who move from place to place. Around 5000 BC, some nomads stopped moving around. They built homes along the Nile River in Egypt. As time went on, a civilization formed.

Each year, starting in June, the Nile River flooded. The high water lasted about four months. It left new soil along the river's banks. This soil reached all the way from the river to about 6 miles (about 9.7 km) inland. Grasses and reeds sprang up. Ducks and geese came to feed on them. Fish swam near the river's shore. The Nile River Valley gave the people what they needed to live.

The pharaoh was the ruler of Egypt. Every man, woman, and child in Egypt had to obey him. When he spoke, his words became law. But there were no rules that he had to follow. He was seen as a god. Brothers and sisters in the pharaoh's family married each other. This kept all the power in one family. One after another, family members would take the throne. A family that holds power this way is called a dynasty. The dynasties in Egypt ruled for many years.

1. What facts and details in the text and picture help you form inferences about ancient Egypt?

   _____

   _____

2. What are the effects of the pharaoh being seen as a god? How do you know?

   _____

   _____

Inferring Question Stems

Use these question stems to develop your own questions for students.

Describe what you already know about _____ (*person/place/ event/time period/concept*).

Identify facts and details the author provides that help you form inferences about _____ (*person/place/event/time period/ concept*).

What key information about _____ (*person/place/event/time period/concept*) is not provided in the text?

Based on what you understand about _____ (*person/place/ event/time period/concept*), predict what would happen if _____ (*event*).

How would the outcome be different if _____ (*person*) had decided to _____ (*action*)?

How do you think _____ (*person/group*) will respond to _____ (*event*)? Which details from the text support your prediction?

Use evidence from the text to describe the effects that result from _____ (*cause/s*).

Read paragraph/sentence _____ on page _____. Based on these ideas, complete the following sentence: If ..., then ....

Based on what you read about _____ (*time period/event*), what conclusions can you draw about _____ (*person/place/ event/concept*)?

Consider the evidence from the text about _____ (*concept*). What conclusions can you draw about life during _____ (*time period/event*)?

Name: _____   Date: _____

Artistic Monuments

Directions: Read this text, and answer the questions.

Perhaps the most notable achievements of the ancient Egyptians are their monuments and artistic work. The size and design of their monuments show much about the talent and ingenuity of these ancient architects. Some of their best-known works are the pyramids.

Pyramids are structures with square bases and four triangular sides that come to a point at the top. Ancient Egyptians used pyramids as tombs. The pyramids were built of granite, limestone, and sandstone. Stone quarries supplied the material. The stones had to precisely fit together because the pyramids were built without mortar between the stones.

Building the enormous pyramids and monuments presented challenges for the Egyptians. A ramp of adobe brick allowed workmen to carry stones to the top of the structures. As height was added, the ramp was raised. Upon completion of the monument, an artist would decorate from the top down. As he continued downward, the ramp was lowered until it was finished.

The art of the ancient Egyptians reflected every aspect of their lives. Their art consisted of scenes from everyday life, family life, and animals. They also made statues, jewelry, glass figures, and containers.

Egyptian pyramids are included among the Seven Wonders of the Ancient World. There are still many ruins of pyramids and monuments standing near the Nile River in Egypt today.

1. What key information about how the pyramids were built is not provided in the text?

   _____

   _____

   _____

2. Consider the evidence from the text about the construction of the pyramids. What conclusions can you draw about life during the time in which they were built?

   _____

   _____

   _____

Inferring Question Stems

Use these question stems to develop your own questions for students.

Explain your current understanding of _____ (*person/place/event/time period/concept*).

Describe the information the author provides to help the reader form inferences about _____ (*person/place/event/time period/concept*).

What key information about _____ (*person/place/event/time period/concept*) is not provided in the text? Why might it be missing?

Predict what would happen if _____ (*event*). How does your understanding about _____ (*person/place/event/time period/concept*) influence your prediction?

Describe an alternative outcome if _____ (*event*) happened differently. Use details from the text to support your position.

Based on your understanding of _____ (*time period/event*), how do you predict _____ (*person/group*) will respond to _____ (*event*)? Use details from the text to support your prediction.

Consider the following details from the text: _____ (*quotation*). If these are causes, what are the effects?

Read paragraph/sentence _____ on page _____. Based on these ideas, complete the following sentence: If ..., then .... Provide evidence to support your statement.

Describe how reading about _____ (*time period/event*) helps you draw conclusions about _____ (*person/place/event/concept*).

Based on the evidence presented in the text about _____ (*concept*), what conclusions can you draw about life during _____ (*time period/event*)?

Name: _____ Date: _____

How Did They Do That?

Directions: Read this text, and study the picture. Then, answer the questions.

The Great Sphinx is possibly one of the most famous and noteworthy monuments in the world. It was built thousands of years ago by the ancient Egyptians. The colossal statue lies in front of Pharaoh Khufu's Great Pyramid at Giza as the pyramid's guardian. This is one of the largest pyramids ever built, and it is one of the Seven Wonders of the Ancient World. Seated at the bedrock of the Giza plateau, the Great Sphinx's head and body are carved from solid rock, and its paws and legs are built of enormous stone blocks. Sand buries its enormous base even though it has been cleared away several times throughout history.

With the body of a lion and the head of a king or a god, the Great Sphinx has come to symbolize strength and wisdom. The size of the Sphinx is monstrous, with a length of 240 feet (73 meters) and height of about 66 feet (20 meters). The width of its face measures 13 feet 8 inches (4.1 meters). Built without the assistance of modern machinery, the Great Sphinx is truly a marvel. Many theories have circulated about how the ancient Egyptians were able to construct such an enormous and complex structure.

Although it is battered in places today, it is believed that the Great Sphinx was once quite colorful. The nose and beard are now broken, and there are varied and contradictory explanations as to how this occurred. Despite the damage and decay that has taken place over thousands of years, the Great Sphinx remains one of the most fantastic and notable achievements of the ancient Egyptians.

1. Describe the information the author provides to help the reader form inferences about the Sphinx guarding the pyramids.

   _____

   _____

2. Describe how reading about the construction of the Sphinx helps you draw conclusions about ancient Egypt.

   _____

   _____

   _____

Inferring K–12 Alignment

Use this chart to determine the best question stems for your different groups of students.

★	●	■	▲
What do you know about _____ (person/place/event/time period/concept)?	What do you already know about _____ (person/place/event/time period/concept)?	Describe what you already know about _____ (person/place/event/time period/concept).	Explain your current understanding of _____ (person/place/event/time period/concept).
What details or pictures in the text help you learn what happened?	What facts and details in the text help you form inferences about _____ (person/place/event/time period/concept)?	Identify facts and details the author provides that help you form inferences about _____ (person/place/event/time period/concept).	Describe the information the author provides to help the reader form inferences about _____ (person/place/event/time period/concept).
What key information is missing from the text?	What key information is not provided in the text?	What key information about _____ (person/place/event/time period/concept) is not provided in the text?	What key information about _____ (person/place/event/time period/concept) is not provided in the text? Why might it be missing?
What do you think would happen if _____ (event)?	Based on what you know about _____ (person/place/event/time period/concept), what do you think would happen if _____ (event)?	Based on what you understand about _____ (person/place/event/time period/concept), predict what would happen if _____ (event).	Predict what would happen if _____ (event). How does your understanding about _____ (person/place/event/time period/concept) influence your prediction?
What would happen if _____ (different outcome)?	How would the outcome change if _____ (event) happened instead?	How would the outcome be different if _____ (person) had decided to _____ (action)?	Describe an alternative outcome if _____ (event) happened differently. Use details from the text to support your position.

Inferring K–12 Alignment (cont.)

★	⬤	◼	▲
What will _____ (*person/group*) do?	How will _____ (*person/group*) respond to _____ (*event*)?	How do you think _____ (*person/group*) will respond to _____ (*event*)? Which details from the text support your prediction?	Based on your understanding of _____ (*time period/event*), how do you predict _____ (*person/group*) will respond to _____ (*event*)? Use details from the text to support your prediction.
What happened after _____ (*cause/s*)?	What are the effects of _____ (*cause/s*)? How do you know?	Use evidence from the text to describe the effects that result from _____ (*cause/s*).	Consider the following details from the text: _____ (*quotation*). If these are causes, what are the effects?
Think about what you read. If _____ (*event*) happened, then what might happen/be true?	Read paragraph/ sentence _____ on page _____. Complete the following sentence: If ..., then	Read paragraph/ sentence _____ on page _____. Based on these ideas, complete the following sentence: If ..., then	Read paragraph/sentence _____ on page _____. Based on these ideas, complete the following sentence: If ..., then .... Provide evidence to support your statement.
What do you know about _____ (*person/place/ event/concept*) now?	After reading about _____ (*time period/ event*), what do you know about _____ (*person/place/ event/concept*)?	Based on what you read about _____ (*time period/event*), what conclusions can you draw about _____ (*person/place/event/ concept*)?	Describe how reading about _____ (*time period/ event*) helps you draw conclusions about _____ (*person/place/event/ concept*).
What was life like during _____ (*time period/event*)?	Think about what you read about _____ (*concept*). What can you say about life during _____ (*time period/ event*)?	Consider the evidence from the text about _____ (*concept*). What conclusions can you draw about life during _____ (*time period/ event*)?	Based on the evidence presented in the text about _____ (*concept*), what conclusions can you draw about life during _____ (*time period/event*)?

Analyzing Perspectives

Skill Overview

Analyzing multiple perspectives is an important skill when studying social studies texts. By analyzing various perspectives, students step outside the text to explore alternative solutions and varying points of view. Students must not only consider the information explicitly stated in the text, but they must also identify personal characteristics and experiences of individuals and groups that may have influenced the text. They must then analyze the text through this lens to determine how these perspectives affected it.

Analyzing perspectives challenges students to consider how one's experiences can contribute to subjectivity and bias. Identifying bias in a text is a key part of this skill. By identifying bias, students can determine which statements or details may have been left out or exaggerated to further the author's point. By considering how one's perspective affects a historical text or primary source, students can learn to apply these principles and skills to texts they encounter in their everyday lives.

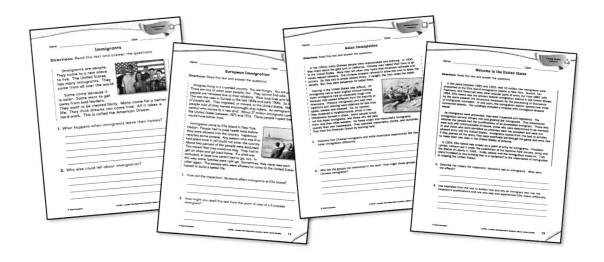

Implementing the Question Stems

This section includes 10 leveled, text-dependent question stems about analyzing perspectives. You can implement these question stems by connecting them to the texts that you are reading in class.

It may seem as though using question stems would be easy, but it can be a complex task for teachers. To help you see how to implement these question stems in your classroom, this section includes student pages containing texts with sample text-dependent questions. Each of the four student pages illustrates a different complexity level.

Snapshot of Differentiating a Question

The chart below models how a single leveled question stem can be tied to social studies texts at four complexity levels. This snapshot also gives a quick view of how the question stems differ based on the complexity levels. However, you can also see how the question stems link to one another.

	Question Stem	Example
☆	Who else could tell about _____ (event/decision)?	Who else could tell about Pilgrims landing in the New World?
○	How might you retell this text from the point of view of _____ (person/group)?	How might you retell this text from the point of view of American Indians?
□	Retell the account of _____ (event/decision) from the point of view of _____ (person/group). How does this change the account?	Retell the account of Anne Frank from the point of view of her mother. How does this change the account?
△	Retell the account of _____ (event/decision) from the point of view of _____ (person/group). Use evidence from the text to describe how this changes the account.	Retell the account of the Battle of Waterloo from the point of view of a soldier. Use evidence from the text to describe how this changes the account.

COMPLEXITY

Analyzing Perspectives Question Stems

Use these question stems to develop your own questions for students.

What would happen if _____ (*person/group*) did _____ (*alternative action*) instead?

Why did the author write/make _____ (*primary source document*)?

Why did _____ (*person*) write/create _____ (*primary source document*)?

What is different about how _____ (*person*) and _____ (*person*) saw _____ (*event*)?

Is anyone not in the text who should be? If so, who?

What would be different if _____ (*person*) were alive today?

What happened when _____ (*person's/group's* decision)?

How might _____ (*person*) react to _____ (*problem*)?

How could you retell _____ (*event/decision*)?

Who else could tell about _____ (*event/decision*)?

Name: _____ Date: _____

Immigrants

Directions: Read this text, and answer the questions.

Immigrants are people. They come to a new place to live. The United States has many immigrants. They come from all over the world.

Some come because it is safer. Some want to get away from bad leaders. They want to be treated fairly. Many come for a better life. They think dreams can come true. All it takes is hard work. This is called the American Dream.

1. What happens when immigrants leave their homes?

_____

_____

_____

_____

_____

2. Who else could tell about immigration?

_____

_____

_____

_____

Analyzing Perspectives Question Stems

Use these question stems to develop your own questions for students.

What would have happened if _____ (*person/group*) and _____ (*person/group*) switched places?

What do you know about the author of _____ (*primary source document*) that may have influenced what he/she wrote/created?

What does the text say about why _____ (*person*) wrote/created _____ (*primary source document*)?

How did _____ (*person*) and _____ (*person*) see _____ (*event*) in different ways?

What person/group is not mentioned in the text that should be? Why might this person/group be left out?

How would _____ (*person*) react differently if he/she were alive today?

How did _____'s (*person/group*) decision affect _____ (*person/group*)?

How might different people or groups react to _____ (*problem*)?

How could you retell what happened during _____ (*event/decision*) to make the point of view more neutral/objective?

How might you retell this text from the point of view of _____ (*person/group*)?

Name: _____ Date: _____

European Immigration

Directions: Read this text, and answer the questions.

Imagine living in a crowded country. You are hungry. You are poor. There are a lot of other poor people, too. They cannot find jobs. Some people are harassed because of their religious beliefs. Wars took lives and land. This was the case in Europe in the late 1800s and early 1900s. So millions of people left. They migrated, or moved, to the United States. Many people sold all they owned and bought ship tickets. An immigrant is a person who moves to a new land. About 27 million immigrants came to the United States between 1870 and 1916. These people hoped they would have better lives.

Immigrants came to Ellis Island in New York Harbor. People had to pass health tests before they were allowed into the country. Inspectors rejected some people. Any person who was ill or had spent time in jail could not enter the country. About two percent of the people were excluded. This meant that they could not stay. They had to get on ships and go back home. If a child was excluded, at least one parent had to go, too. In this way, some families were split up. Sometimes, they never saw each other again. The people who were allowed to come to the United States hoped to build a better life.

1. How did the inspectors' decisions affect immigrants at Ellis Island?

_____

_____

2. How might you retell this text from the point of view of a European immigrant?

_____

_____

Analyzing Perspectives Question Stems

Use these question stems to develop your own questions for students.

How might history have been different if _____ (*person/group*) and _____ (*person/group*) switched roles?

What evidence is there that the author's experiences shaped the perspective of _____ (*primary source document*)?

Explain the historical events that happened around the time _____ (*person*) wrote/created _____ (*primary source document*). How might that have affected the author's perspective?

Describe how _____ (*person*) and _____ (*person*) experienced _____ (*event*) differently.

Who are the people/groups not mentioned in the text? How might this person/group feel about _____ (*person/place/event/time period/concept*)?

Use evidence from the text to explain how _____'s (*person*) perspective might be different if he/she were alive today.

Explain how _____'s (*person/group*) decision impacted _____ (*person/group*).

How might various people or groups respond to the problem caused by _____ (*person/group*)?

Rewrite/rephrase this account of _____ (*event/decision*), limiting any bias.

Retell the account of _____ (*event/decision*) from the point of view of _____ (*person/group*). How does this change the account?

Name: _____ Date: _____

Asian Immigration

Directions: Read this text, and answer the questions.

In the 1800s, many Chinese people were impoverished and starving. In 1850, they heard about the gold rush in California. Chinese men risked their lives to go to the United States. More men left when they heard that American railroads and mines needed laborers. The Chinese emperor refused to allow the men to leave the country. So they had to sneak aboard ships. If caught, the men faced the death penalty. But, they were desperate for better lives.

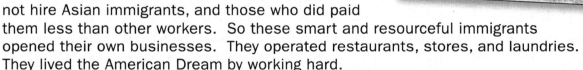

Coming to the United States was difficult. All immigrants had to learn English without training. Asian immigrants had an especially tough time because they looked different from the majority of Americans. Chinese immigrants who kept their traditions and clothing were attacked for how they spoke, looked, and dressed. So, for comfort, they clustered in neighborhoods, which is how Chinatowns formed in cities. Some people would not hire Asian immigrants, and those who did paid them less than other workers. So these smart and resourceful immigrants opened their own businesses. They operated restaurants, stores, and laundries. They lived the American Dream by working hard.

1. Describe how Chinese immigrants and white Americans experienced the rise of Asian immigration differently.

   _____

   _____

   _____

2. Who are the groups not mentioned in the text? How might these groups feel about Chinese immigrants?

   _____

   _____

   _____

   _____

Analyzing Perspectives Question Stems

Use these question stems to develop your own questions for students.

Hypothesize how history would have been different if _____ (*person/group*) and _____ (*person/group*) reversed roles.

What evidence exists that the author's personal characteristics or experiences shaped the perspective of _____ (*primary source document*)?

Provide examples from the text of how the author's personal experiences or current events impacted his/her objectivity while writing/creating _____ (*primary source document*).

Use examples from the text to explain how/why _____ (*person*) and _____ (*person*) experienced _____ (*event*) differently.

Explain which important people/groups are not mentioned in the text. Why are they not included? What might their opinions about _____ (*person/place/event/time period/concept*) be?

Use evidence and details from the text to describe how _____'s (*person*) perspective would be different if he/she were alive today.

Describe the impact that _____'s (*person/group*) decision had on _____ (*person/group*). What were the effects?

Describe the ways various people or groups might react differently to the problem caused by _____ (*person/group*).

Determine the bias in the text. Rewrite/rephrase the account of _____ (*event/decision*) to make it more objective.

Retell the account of _____ (*event/decision*) from the point of view of _____ (*person/group*). Use evidence from the text to describe how this changes the account.

Name: _____ Date: _____

Welcome to the United States

Directions: Read this text, and answer the questions.

In the years between 1892 and 1922, over 12 million new immigrants were processed at the Ellis Island immigration station in New York. Boston, San Francisco, and Savannah were other popular ports of entry. But from 1892 until 1954, Ellis Island was the primary federal immigration station in the United States. As the years passed, the structures necessary for the processing of thousands of immigrants increased. At one point, the immigration station spread over three connected islands. The buildings included a hospital with contagious disease wards.

As immigrants were processed, they were inspected and registered. The immigration service officers met and greeted the immigrants. They determined whether the people met the qualifications of an acceptable immigrant. Those who were sick with communicable illnesses, those who were determined to be mentally ill, and those who were identified as criminals were not accepted and were not allowed entry into the United States. Immigrants moved from one test to another. If they passed all the tests, they were eventually led through the gates and were free to make their new lives in the United States of America.

In 1954, Ellis Island was closed as a point of entry for immigrants. President Lyndon Johnson put it under the jurisdiction of the National Park Service, along with the Statue of Liberty in 1965. Today, people visit the immigration museum. They stand humbled by this building that is a testament to how immigration shaped the United States.

1. Describe the impact the inspectors' decisions had on immigrants. What were the effects?

   _____

   _____

   _____

2. Use examples from the text to explain how an immigrant who met the inspector's qualifications experienced Ellis Island differently than one who was sick.

   _____

   _____

   _____

   _____

Analyzing Perspectives K–12 Alignment

Use this chart to determine the best question stems for your different groups of students.

★	●	■	▲
What would happen if _____ (*person/group*) did _____ (*alternative action*) instead?	What would have happened if _____ (*person/group*) and _____ (*person/group*) switched places?	How might history have been different if _____ (*person/group*) and _____ (*person/group*) switched roles?	Hypothesize how history would have been different if _____ (*person/group*) and _____ (*person/group*) reversed roles.
Why did the author write/make _____ (*primary source document*)?	What do you know about the author of _____ (*primary source document*) that may have influenced what he/she wrote/created?	What evidence is there that the author's experiences shaped the perspective of _____ (*primary source document*)?	What evidence exists that the author's personal characteristics or experiences shaped the perspective of _____ (*primary source document*)?
Why did _____ (*person*) write/create _____ (*primary source document*)?	What does the text say about why _____ (*person*) wrote/created _____ (*primary source document*)?	Explain the historical events that happened around the time _____ (*person*) wrote/created _____ (*primary source document*). How might that have affected the author's perspective?	Provide examples from the text of how the author's personal experiences or current events impacted his/her objectivity while writing/creating _____ (*primary source document*).
What is different about how _____ (*person*) and _____ (*person*) saw _____ (*event*)?	How did _____ (*person*) and _____ (*person*) see _____ (*event*) in different ways?	Describe how _____ (*person*) and _____ (*person*) experienced _____ (*event*) differently.	Use examples from the text to explain how/why _____ (*person*) and _____ (*person*) experienced _____ (*event*) differently.
Is anyone not in the text who should be? If so, who?	What person/group is not mentioned in the text that should be? Why might this person/group be left out?	Who are the people/groups not mentioned in the text? How might this person/group feel about _____ (*person/place/event/time period/concept*)?	Explain which important people/groups are not mentioned in the text. Why are they not included? What might their opinions about _____ (*person/place/event/time period/concept*) be?

Analyzing Perspectives K–12 Alignment *(cont.)*

★	●	■	▲
What would be different if _____ (*person*) were alive today?	How would _____ (*person*) react differently if he/she were alive today?	Use evidence from the text to explain how _____'s (*person*) perspective might be different if he/she were alive today.	Use evidence and details from the text to describe how _____'s (*person*) perspective would be different if he/she were alive today.
What happened when _____ (*person's/group's decision*)?	How did _____'s (*person/group*) decision affect _____ (*person/group*)?	Explain how _____'s (*person/group*) decision impacted _____ (*person/group*).	Describe the impact that _____'s (*person/group*) decision had on _____ (*person/group*). What were the effects?
How might _____ (*person*) react to _____ (*problem*)?	How might different people or groups react to _____ (*problem*)?	How might various people or groups respond to the problem caused by _____ (*person/group*)?	Describe the ways various people or groups might react differently to the problem caused by _____ (*person/group*).
How could you retell _____ (*event/decision*)?	How could you retell what happened during _____ (*event/decision*) to make the point of view more neutral/objective?	Rewrite/rephrase this account of _____ (*event/decision*), limiting any bias.	Determine the bias in the text. Rewrite/rephrase the account of _____ (*event/decision*) to make it more objective.
Who else could tell about _____ (*event/decision*)?	How might you retell this text from the point of view of _____ (*person/group*)?	Retell the account of _____ (*event/decision*) from the point of view of _____ (*person/group*). How does this change the account?	Retell the account of _____ (*event/decision*) from the point of view of _____ (*person/group*). Use evidence from the text to describe how this changes the account.

Analyzing Change and Continuity

Skill Overview

Another key social studies skill is analyzing change and continuity. Students study how ideas and concepts have changed and remained the same over periods of time. They identify events that preceded and succeeded an event or time period. They also describe the causes and effects of events on later events and time periods. This includes assessing the magnitude of change and the nature of impact. An impact may be positive, negative, or both. Impacts can be long term or short term, and students should be able to identify both kinds.

Analyzing change and continuity also provides the opportunity to study how past events shape our present experiences. This skill helps students understand the importance of sequencing and chronology as well as recognizing patterns across time and space.

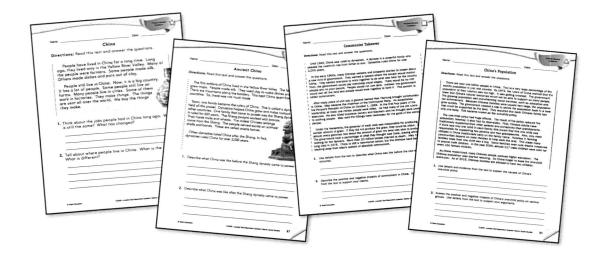

Implementing the Question Stems

This section includes 10 leveled, text-dependent question stems about analyzing change and continuity. You can implement these question stems by connecting them to the texts that you are reading in class.

It may seem as though using question stems would be easy, but it can be a complex task for teachers. To help you see how to implement these question stems in your classroom, this section includes student pages containing texts with sample text-dependent questions. Each of the four student pages illustrates a different complexity level.

Snapshot of Differentiating a Question

The chart below models how a single leveled question stem can be tied to social studies texts at four complexity levels. This snapshot also gives a quick view of how the question stems differ based on the complexity levels. However, you can also see how the question stems link to one another.

	Question Stem	Example
☆	What was _____ (*person/location*) like before _____ (*event*)?	What was the country like before cars were invented?
○	Describe what _____ (*person/location*) was like before _____ (*event*).	Describe what the country was like before the telephone was invented.
□	Use details from the text to describe what _____ (*person/location*) was like before _____ (*event*) occurred.	Use details from the text to describe what the United States was like before the Civil War occurred.
△	Use details from the text to describe what _____ (*person/location*) was like before _____ (*event*) occurred and what caused the change.	Use details from the text to describe what life in Europe was like before the Renaissance occurred and what caused the change.

Analyzing Change and Continuity Question Stems

Use these question stems to develop your own questions for students.

What was _____ (*person/location*) like before _____ (*event*)?

What was _____ (*person/location*) like after _____ (*event*)?

What happened before _____ (*event/time period*)?

What happened after _____ (*event/time period*)?

Why did _____ (*event*) happen?

Was the result of _____ (*event*) good? Why or why not?

Think about _____ (*event/time period*). What is still the same?
What has changed?

Think about _____ (*person/concept*) during _____ (*time period*). What is still the same? What has changed?

Think about the steps used to/for _____ (*process*) during _____ (*time period*). What is still the same? What has changed?

Tell about _____ (*concept*). What is the same? What is different?

Name: _____   Date: _____

China

Directions: Read this text, and answer the questions.

People have lived in China for a long time. Long ago, they lived only in the Yellow River Valley. Many of the people were farmers. Some people made silk. Others made dishes and pots out of clay.

People still live in China. Now, it is a big country. It has a lot of people. Some people still live on farms. Many people live in cities. Some of them work in factories. They make things. The things are sent all over the world. We buy the things they make.

1. Think about the jobs people had in China long ago. What is still the same? What has changed?

   _____

   _____

   _____

   _____

2. Tell about where people live in China. What is the same? What is different?

   _____

   _____

   _____

   _____

Analyzing Change and Continuity Question Stems

Use these question stems to develop your own questions for students.

Describe what _____ (*person/location*) was like before _____ (*event*).

Describe what _____ (*person/location*) was like after _____ (*event*).

Describe the events that happened before _____ (*event/ time period*).

Describe the events that happened after _____ (*event/ time period*).

Describe the cause of _____ (*event*).

Was the impact of _____ (*event*) positive or negative? Support your opinion with details from the text.

Think about _____ (*event/time period*). What is the same? What has changed? Why?

Think about _____ (*person/concept*) during _____ (*time period*) versus today. What is the same? What has changed? Why?

Think about the steps used to/for _____ (*process*) during _____ (*time period*) and the steps used today. What is the same? What has changed? Why?

Describe _____ (*concept*) and how it changed over time. Why did it change?

Name: _____ Date: _____

Ancient China

Directions: Read this text, and answer the questions.

The first settlers of China lived in the Yellow River Valley. The farmers grew crops. People made silk. They used clay to make dishes and pots. There are mountains along the borders. This kept China apart from other countries. So, there was not much trade.

Soon, one family became the rulers of China. The family held all the power. This is called a dynasty. Dynasties helped China grow and make contact with other countries. One family that came to power was the Shang dynasty. It ruled for 600 years. The Shang people worked with bronze. They made tools and wheels. The oldest Chinese writings come from the Shang dynasty. The people carved words on animals' shells and bones. These are called oracle bones.

Other dynasties ruled China after the Shang. In fact, dynasties ruled China for over 2,000 years.

1. Describe what China was like before the Shang dynasty came to power.

_____

_____

_____

2. Describe what China was like after the Shang dynasty came to power.

_____

_____

_____

Analyzing Change and Continuity Question Stems

Use these question stems to develop your own questions for students.

Use details from the text to describe what _____ (*person/ location*) was like before _____ (*event*) occurred.

- -

Use details from the text to describe what _____ (*person/ location*) was like after _____ (*event*) occurred.

- -

Use details from the text to describe the events that led up to _____ (*event/time period*).

- -

What was the immediate impact of _____ (*event/time period*)?

- -

How does the text describe the cause(s) of _____ (*event*)?

- -

Describe the positive and negative impacts of _____ (*event*). Use details from the text to support your claims.

- -

Consider _____ (*event/time period*). What has remained the same, and what has changed? Use the text to explain why.

- -

Consider _____ (*person/concept*) during _____ (*time period*). How is it similar to and different from _____ (*person/concept*) today?

- -

Think about the steps used to/for _____ (*process*) during _____ (*time period*). How is it similar to and different from the steps used today?

- -

Trace the development of _____ (*concept*) from _____ (*year/ time period*) to _____ (*year/time period*). What has changed? What has remained the same?

Name: _____ Date: _____

Communist Takeover

Directions: Read this text, and answer the questions.

Until 1949, China was ruled by dynasties. A dynasty is a powerful family who passes the country's rule from father to son. Dynasties ruled China for over 2,000 years.

In the early 1900s, many Chinese workers and peasants started to dream about a new kind of government. They wanted a system where the people would control China. They wanted everyone to work together to do what was best for the country. Then, the government would pay everybody equal wages. There would be no rich people and no poor people. People would not own land. Instead, the government would own all the land and people would work together to farm it. This system is called communism.

After many years of civil war, a general named Mao Tse-tung brought communism to China. Mao became the chairman of the Communist Party. He established the People's Republic of China on October 1, 1949. In the first four years of his leadership, at least one million people were killed. He had many of the old rulers executed. He also killed business owners and teachers who he thought were unkind to working people. Mao said the killings were necessary for the good of the working people.

Under his leadership, the governor of each area was responsible for producing a certain amount of grain. If they did not produce the grain, they could be killed. So almost every governor lied about the amount of grain his area was able to produce. The government took a percentage of what they thought was there, leaving almost nothing for the farmers. More than 20 million people starved to death. Mao Tse-tung died in 1976. China is still a communist nation, but the Chinese have been backing away from Mao's system of absolute communism.

1. Use details from the text to describe what China was like before the civil war occurred.

   _____

   _____

2. Describe the positive and negative impacts of communism in China. Use details from the text to support your claims.

   _____

   _____

Analyzing Change and Continuity
Question Stems

Use these question stems to develop your own questions for students.

Use details from the text to describe what _____ (*person/ location*) was like before _____ (*event*) occurred and what caused the change.

Use details from the text to describe what _____ (*person/ location*) was like after _____ (*event*) occurred and what caused the change.

Use details and evidence from the text to explain the significant events that led up to _____ (*event/time period*).

What was the immediate impact of _____ (*event/time period*)? What was its long-term impact?

Use evidence from the text to explain the cause(s) of _____ (*event*).

Assess the positive and negative impacts of _____ (*event*) on various people/groups. Use details from the text to support your arguments.

Consider _____ (*event/time period*). Use evidence from the text to describe what has changed, what has remained the same, and why.

Compare and contrast the role of _____ (*person/concept*) during _____ (*time period*) and the role of _____ (*person/ concept*) in the present day.

Consider the steps used to/for _____ (*process*) during _____ (*time period*). Compare and contrast this to the steps used today.

Trace the development of _____ (*concept*) from _____ (*year/ time period*) to _____ (*year/time period*). Describe how this concept has changed over time and what has remained the same.

Name: _____ Date: _____

China's Population

Directions: Read this text, and answer the questions.

There are over one billion people in China. This is a very large percentage of the world's population in just one country. By 1979, the rulers of China worried that the population of their country was too high. It was getting crowded. The government knew that China's natural resources would not be able to support so many people. The growing population was overwhelming social services, such as education and law enforcement. Because Chinese families were usually very large, the population grew quickly. The government needed a way to shrink the population back to a level that could be supported by the land. They required that each Chinese family had only one baby. This became known as the one-child policy.

The one-child policy had huge effects. The policy did manage to reduce the population; however, it also had its downsides. First, Chinese adults have traditionally supported their older parents and sometimes their grandparents. If there was only one child in each family, this meant that this one child was responsible for supporting two parents and four grandparents. Also, only male children in China traditionally carry on the family name. Families in farming communities depend on male children to help work the land. This made many families hope their one child was a boy. Some families even took drastic measures to ensure male children. In the year 2000, almost 117 male children were born for every 100 female children.

As China modernized, many Chinese people pursued higher education. The Chinese population also started reducing. So China began to ease the one-child restriction. As of 2016, Chinese families are allowed to have two children.

1. Use details and evidence from the text to explain the causes of China's one-child policy.

_____

_____

_____

2. Assess the positive and negative impacts of China's one-child policy on various groups. Use details from the text to support your arguments.

_____

_____

_____

Analyzing Change and Continuity
K–12 Alignment

Use this chart to determine the best question stems for your different groups of students.

★	●	■	▲
What was _____ (person/location) like before _____ (event)?	Describe what _____ (person/location) was like before _____ (event).	Use details from the text to describe what _____ (person/location) was like before _____ (event) occurred.	Use details from the text to describe what _____ (person/location) was like before _____ (event) occurred and what caused the change.
What was _____ (person/location) like after _____ (event)?	Describe what _____ (person/location) was like after _____ (event).	Use details from the text to describe what _____ (person/location) was like after _____ (event) occurred.	Use details from the text to describe what _____ (person/location) was like after _____ (event) occurred and what caused the change.
What happened before _____ (event/time period)?	Describe the events that happened before _____ (event/time period).	Use details from the text to describe the events that led up to _____ (event/time period).	Use details and evidence from the text to explain the significant events that led up to _____ (event/time period).
What happened after _____ (event/time period)?	Describe the events that happened after _____ (event/time period).	What was the immediate impact of _____ (event/time period)?	What was the immediate impact of _____ (event/time period)? What was its long-term impact?
Why did _____ (event) happen?	Describe the cause of _____ (event).	How does the text describe the cause(s) of _____ (event)?	Use evidence from the text to explain the cause(s) of _____ (event).
Was the result of _____ (event) good? Why or why not?	Was the impact of _____ (event) positive or negative? Support your opinion with details from the text.	Describe the positive and negative impacts of _____ (event). Use details from the text to support your claims.	Assess the positive and negative impacts of _____ (event) on various people/groups. Use details from the text to support your arguments.

Analyzing Change and Continuity
K–12 Alignment (cont.)

★	●	■	▲
Think about _____ (*event/time period*). What is still the same? What has changed?	Think about _____ (*event/time period*). What is the same? What has changed? Why?	Consider _____ (*event/time period*). What has remained the same, and what has changed? Use the text to explain why.	Consider _____ (*event/ time period*). Use evidence from the text to describe what has changed, what has remained the same, and why.
Think about _____ (*person/concept*) during _____ (*time period*). What is still the same? What has changed?	Think about _____ (*person/concept*) during _____ (*time period*) versus today. What is the same? What has changed? Why?	Consider _____ (*person/concept*) during _____ (*time period*). How is it similar to and different from _____ (*person/concept*) today?	Compare and contrast the role of _____ (*person/ concept*) during _____ (*time period*) and the role of _____ (*person/concept*) in the present day.
Think about the steps used to/for _____ (*process*) during _____ (*time period*). What is still the same? What has changed?	Think about the steps used to/for _____ (*process*) during _____ (*time period*) and the steps used today. What is the same? What has changed? Why?	Think about the steps used to/for _____ (*process*) during _____ (*time period*). How is it similar to and different from the steps used today?	Consider the steps used to/for _____ (*process*) during _____ (*time period*). Compare and contrast this to the steps used today.
Tell about _____ (*concept*). What is the same? What is different?	Describe _____ (*concept*) and how it changed over time. Why did it change?	Trace the development of _____ (*concept*) from _____ (*year/ time period*) to _____ (*year/time period*). What has changed? What has remained the same?	Trace the development of _____ (*concept*) from _____ (*year/time period*) to _____ (*year/time period*). Describe how this concept has changed over time and what has remained the same.

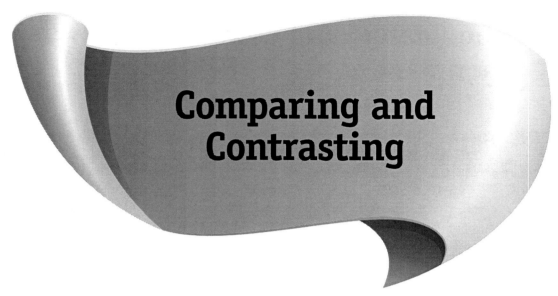

Comparing and Contrasting

Skill Overview

Comparing and contrasting are essential social studies skills that can be applied in a wide range of contexts. When comparing, students find similarities among people, places, events, time periods, or concepts. The skill of contrasting requires students to distinguish between people, places, events, time periods, or concepts by examining differing characteristics or features. Students can also consider how events and people from long ago are similar to and different from events and people today. Students identify how concepts can be compared and contrasted to other texts that they have read. An important aspect of comparing and contrasting is the ability to categorize similarities and differences. This requires students to think more deeply about how ideas are similar and different. The application of these skills allows teachers to assess deeper levels of comprehension and build conceptual understanding of the text itself and the time period being studied.

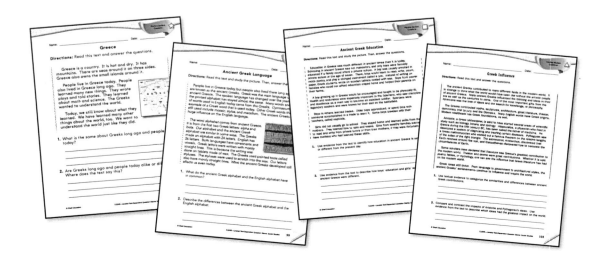

Implementing the Question Stems

This section includes 10 leveled, text-dependent question stems about comparing and contrasting. You can implement these question stems by connecting them to the texts that you are reading in class.

It may seem as though using question stems would be easy, but it can be a complex task for teachers. To help you see how to implement these question stems in your classroom, this section includes student pages containing texts with sample text-dependent questions. Each of the four student pages illustrates a different complexity level.

Snapshot of Differentiating a Question

The chart below models how a single leveled question stem can be tied to social studies texts at four complexity levels. This snapshot also gives a quick view of how the question stems differ based on the complexity levels. However, you can also see how the question stems link to one another.

	Question Stem	Example
☆	Are _____ (concept) and _____ (concept) alike or different? Where does the text say this?	Is life in the city and life in the country alike or different? Where does the text say this?
○	How are _____ (concept) and _____ (concept) compared/contrasted in the text?	How are government leaders and community leaders compared in the text?
□	What key words indicate that the author has structured the text to compare/contrast _____ (concept) and _____ (concept)?	What key words indicate that the author has structured the text to contrast the legislative and the judicial branches of the government?
△	Describe the ways in which the author structured the text to compare/contrast _____ (concept) and _____ (concept).	Describe the ways in which the author structured the text to compare national and global economies.

Comparing and Contrasting Question Stems

Use these question stems to develop your own questions for students.

Are _____ (*concept*) and _____ (*concept*) alike or different? Where does the text say this?

What is the same about _____ (*person/place/event/time period/concept*) and _____ (*person/place/event/time period/concept*)?

What is the difference between _____ (*person/place/event/time period/concept*) and _____ (*person/place/event/time period/concept*)?

How did _____ (*person/group*) react to _____ (*event*)? How did _____ (*other person/group*) react?

What was the result of _____ (*concept/event*)? What was the result of _____ (*other concept/event*)?

Can _____ (*person/place/concept*) be called _____ (*category*)? Why or why not?

How is _____ (*person/place/event/time period/concept*) the same as/different from what you already knew?

What is the same/different about _____ (*person/place/event/time period/concept*) and today?

How does the text tell that _____ (*person/place/concept*) and _____ (*person/place/concept*) are the same?

How does the text tell that _____ (*person/place/concept*) and _____ (*person/place/concept*) are different?

Name: _____   Date: _____

Greece

Directions: Read this text, and answer the questions.

Greece is a country. It is hot and dry. It has mountains. There are seas around it on three sides. Greece also owns the small islands around it.

People live in Greece today. People also lived in Greece long ago. They learned many new things. They wrote plays and told stories. They learned about math and science. The Greeks wanted to understand the world.

Today, we still know about what they learned. We have learned many other things about the world, too. We want to understand the world just like they did.

1. What is the same about Greeks long ago and people today?

_____

_____

_____

2. Are Greeks long ago and people today alike or different? Where does the text say this?

_____

_____

_____

Comparing and Contrasting Question Stems

Use these question stems to develop your own questions for students.

How are _____ (*concept*) and _____ (*concept*) compared/ contrasted in the text?

What do _____ (*person/place/event/time period/concept*) and _____ (*person/place/event/time period/concept*) have in common?

Describe the differences between _____ (*person/place/event/ time period/concept*) and _____ (*person/place/event/time period/concept*).

How were the reactions of _____ (*person/group*) and _____ (*person/group*) to _____ (*event*) similar? How were their reactions different?

Describe the impact of _____ (*concept/event*) and _____ (*concept/event*).

What is one way to categorize the similarities/differences between _____ (*person/place/concept*) and _____ (*person/ place/concept*)?

How is _____ (*person/place/event/time period/concept*) similar to/different from other texts you have read about this?

How is _____ (*person/place/event/time period/concept*) the same as today? How is it different? Use the text to explain your answer.

How does the text explain that _____ (*person/place/concept*) and _____ (*person/place/concept*) are the same?

How does the text explain that _____ (*person/place/concept*) and _____ (*person/place/concept*) are different?

Name: _____ Date: _____

Ancient Greek Language

Directions: Read this text, and study the picture. Then, answer the questions.

People live in Greece today, but people also lived there long ago. They are known as the ancient Greeks. Greek was the main language used in ancient Greece. The spoken language has changed over the years. But the printed alphabet has stayed almost the same. Many words and parts of words used in English today came from the ancient Greeks. *Gymnasium* is an example of a Greek word that is used today. Other Greek words that are still used include *mosaic, stylus,* and *marathon.* The ancient Greeks had a huge influence on the English language.

The word *alphabet* comes from ancient Greece. It is from the first two Greek letters: *alpha* and *beta.* Our alphabet and the Greek alphabet are similar in some ways. The ancient Greeks made an alphabet with 24 letters. English has 26 letters. Both languages have consonants and vowels. Greek letters were written with mostly straight lines. This is because the writing was done on tablets made of wax. The ancient Greeks used pointed tools called styluses. The styluses were used to scratch into the wax. Our letters also have mostly straight lines. What the ancient Greeks developed still affects us even today.

1. What do the ancient Greek alphabet and the English alphabet have in common?

   _____

   _____

2. Describe the differences between the ancient Greek alphabet and the English alphabet.

   _____

   _____

Comparing and Contrasting Question Stems

Use these question stems to develop your own questions for students.

What key words indicate that the author has structured the text to compare/contrast _____ (*concept*) and _____ (*concept*)?

Describe the key characteristics that _____ (*person/place/event/time period/concept*) and _____ (*person/place/event/time period/concept*) have in common.

Use evidence from the text to describe how _____ (*person/place/event/time period/concept*) and _____ (*person/place/event/time period/concept*) are different.

Explain how the reactions of _____ (*person/group*) and _____ (*person/group*) to _____ (*event*) were similar and different.

Compare and contrast the impacts of _____ (*concept/event*) and _____ (*concept/event*). Which concept/event had the greatest impact on _____ (*person/group*)?

Use examples from the text to categorize the similarities and/or differences between _____ (*person/place/concept*) and _____ (*person/place/concept*).

Compare and contrast _____ (*person/place/event/time period/concept*) with other texts you have read on the same topic.

Use evidence from the text to identify how _____ (*person/place/event/time period/concept*) is similar to or different from the present day.

Use the text to show how the author compares _____ (*person/place/concept*) and _____ (*person/place/concept*).

Use the text to show how the author contrasts _____ (*person/place/concept*) and _____ (*person/place/concept*).

Name: _____ Date: _____

Ancient Greek Education

Directions: Read this text. Then, answer the questions.

Education in ancient Greece was much different than it is today. Schooling in ancient Greece was not mandatory, and only boys were formally educated if their families could afford private school. Boys were usually enrolled in private school at the age of seven. There, boys would learn to read, write, count, recite poetry, and play a stringed instrument called a lyre. Instead of writing on paper, Greek students wrote on wooden tablets coated with wax. Boys from poorer families who could not afford education stayed home and helped their parents on their farms.

A boy growing up in Greece would be encouraged and taught to be physically fit. Health and endurance were especially important to the Spartans, who saw discipline and obedience as the main way to become an excellent soldier. Spartans were legendary soldiers and were known for their skill on the battlefield.

Boys in Athens learned trades. Older boys apprenticed, or spent time with someone accomplished in a trade to learn it. Some boys traveled with their teachers, called sophists.

Girls did not usually go to school. They stayed home and learned skills from their mothers. They learned how to spin and weave. Girls from wealthy families learned to read and write from private tutors or from their mothers, if they were fortunate to have mothers who had learned these skills.

1. Use evidence from the text to identify how education in ancient Greece is similar to or different from the present day.

   _____

   _____

   _____

2. Use evidence from the text to describe how boys' education and girls' education in ancient Greece were different.

   _____

   _____

   _____

Comparing and Contrasting Question Stems

Use these question stems to develop your own questions for students.

Describe the ways in which the author structured the text to compare/contrast _____ (*concept*) and _____ (*concept*).

Outline the key characteristics and details that _____ (*person/place/event/time period/concept*) and _____ (*person/place/event/time period/concept*) have in common.

Use evidence and details from the text to explain how _____ (*person/place/event/time period/concept*) and _____ (*person/place/event/time period/concept*) are different and why.

Compare and contrast the reactions that _____ (*person/group*) and _____ (*person/group*) had to _____ (*event*).

Compare and contrast the impacts of _____ (*concept/event*) and _____ (*concept/event*). Use evidence from the text to describe which concept/event had the greatest impact on _____ (*person/group*).

Use textual evidence to categorize the similarities and/or differences between _____ (*person/place/concept*) and _____ (*person/place/concept*).

Use evidence from the text to compare and contrast _____ (*person/place/event/time period/concept*) with other texts you have read on this topic or a similar one.

Compare and contrast _____ (*person/place/event/time period/concept*) to the present day. Use evidence from the text to explain similarities and differences.

Use specific evidence from the text to identify how the author compares _____ (*person/place/concept*) and _____ (*person/place/concept*).

Use specific evidence from the text to identify how the author contrasts _____ (*person/place/concept*) and _____ (*person/place/concept*).

Name: _____ Date: _____

Greek Influence

Directions: Read this text, and answer the questions.

The ancient Greeks contributed to many different fields in the modern world. It is strange to think what the world would have been like without the artistic people of ancient Greece. Many ancient Greeks influenced the thinking and ideas in their era as well as in the centuries to come.

The Greeks contributed myths, sculptures, architecture, great literature, theater, democracy, trial by jury, and the Olympics. Many English words have Greek origins. Modern health care has Greek foundations, as well. One of the most important gifts from the Athenians was the search for knowledge, or philosophy.

Aristotle, a Greek philosopher, is said to have started several areas of scientific study, such as biology, botany, and zoology. Hippocrates, a physician who lived in Greece during the fifth century BC, has been called the father of medicine. He developed a system of diagnosing and treating certain diseases. Pythagoras was a Greek mathematician who worked out a famous theorem on the relative lengths of the sides of the right triangle. The astronomer Aristarchus discovered that Earth revolves around the sun, and Eratosthenes discovered how to calculate the circumference of Earth.

Some scholars have declared that literature was Greece's greatest contribution to the modern world. Theater and drama were great contributions. Whether it is epic poetry, fables, or mythology, one can see the influence that Greek literature has had on the modern world.

Greek ideas still thrive. From language to government to architectural styles, the ancient Greeks' achievements continue to influence and inspire the world.

1. Use textual evidence to categorize the similarities or differences between various Greek contributions.

_____

_____

_____

2. Compare and contrast the impacts of Aristotle's and Pythagoras's ideas. Use evidence from the text to describe which ideas had the greatest impact on the world.

_____

_____

Comparing and Contrasting K–12 Alignment

Use this chart to determine the best question stems for your different groups of students.

★	●	■	▲
Are _____ (concept) and _____ (concept) alike or different? Where does the text say this?	How are _____ (concept) and _____ (concept) compared/ contrasted in the text?	What key words indicate that the author has structured the text to compare/ contrast _____ (concept) and _____ (concept)?	Describe the ways in which the author structured the text to compare/contrast _____ (concept) and _____ (concept).
What is the same about _____ (person/place/ event/time period/ concept) and _____ (person/place/ event/time period/ concept)?	What do _____ (person/place/ event/time period/ concept) and _____ (person/place/ event/time period/ concept) have in common?	Describe the key characteristics that _____ (person/place/ event/time period/ concept) and _____ (person/place/event/ time period/concept) have in common.	Outline the key characteristics and details that _____ (person/place/ event/time period/concept) and _____ (person/place/ event/time period/concept) have in common.
What is the difference between _____ (person/ place/event/time period/concept) and _____ (person/ place/event/time period/concept)?	Describe the differences between _____ (person/place/ event/time period/ concept) and _____ (person/place/ event/time period/ concept).	Use evidence from the text to describe how _____ (person/ place/event/time period/concept) and _____ (person/place/ event/time period/ concept) are different.	Use evidence and details from the text to explain how _____ (person/place/ event/time period/concept) and _____ (person/place/ event/time period/concept) are different and why.
How did _____ (person/group) react to _____ (event)? How did _____ (other person/group) react?	How were the reactions of _____ (person/group) and _____ (person/ group) to _____ (event) similar? How were their reactions different?	Explain how the reactions of _____ (person/group) and _____ (person/group) to _____ (event) were similar and different.	Compare and contrast the reactions that _____ (person/group) and _____ (person/group) had to _____ (event).
What was the result of _____ (concept/ event)? What was the result of _____ (other concept/ event)?	Describe the impact of _____ (concept/event) and _____ (concept/ event).	Compare and contrast the impacts of _____ (concept/event) and _____ (concept/ event). Which concept/event had the greatest impact on _____ (person/ group)?	Compare and contrast the impacts of _____ (concept/event) and _____ (concept/event). Use evidence from the text to describe which concept/ event had the greatest impact on _____ (person/ group).

Comparing and Contrasting K–12 Alignment (cont.)

★	●	■	▲
Can _____ (*person/place/concept*) be called _____ (*category*)? Why or why not?	What is one way to categorize the similarities/differences between _____ (*person/place/concept*) and _____ (*person/place/concept*)?	Use examples from the text to categorize the similarities and/or differences between _____ (*person/place/concept*) and _____ (*person/place/concept*).	Use textual evidence to categorize the similarities and/or differences between _____ (*person/place/concept*) and _____ (*person/place/concept*).
How is _____ (*person/place/event/time period/concept*) the same as/different from what you already knew?	How is _____ (*person/place/event/time period/concept*) similar to/different from other texts you have read about this?	Compare and contrast _____ (*person/place/event/time period/concept*) with other texts you have read on the same topic.	Use evidence from the text to compare and contrast _____ (*person/place/event/time period/concept*) with other texts you have read on this topic or a similar one.
What is the same/different about _____ (*person/place/event/time period/concept*) and today?	How is _____ (*person/place/event/time period/concept*) the same as today? How is it different? Use the text to explain your answer.	Use evidence from the text to identify how _____ (*person/place/event/time period/concept*) is similar to or different from the present day.	Compare and contrast _____ (*person/place/event/time period/concept*) to the present day. Use evidence from the text to explain similarities and differences.
How does the text tell that _____ (*person/place/concept*) and _____ (*person/place/concept*) are the same?	How does the text explain that _____ (*person/place/concept*) and _____ (*person/place/concept*) are the same?	Use the text to show how the author compares _____ (*person/place/concept*) and _____ (*person/place/concept*).	Use specific evidence from the text to identify how the author compares _____ (*person/place/concept*) and _____ (*person/place/concept*).
How does the text tell that _____ (*person/place/concept*) and _____ (*person/place/concept*) are different?	How does the text explain that _____ (*person/place/concept*) and _____ (*person/place/concept*) are different?	Use the text to show how the author contrasts _____ (*person/place/concept*) and _____ (*person/place/concept*).	Use specific evidence from the text to identify how the author contrasts _____ (*person/place/concept*) and _____ (*person/place/concept*).

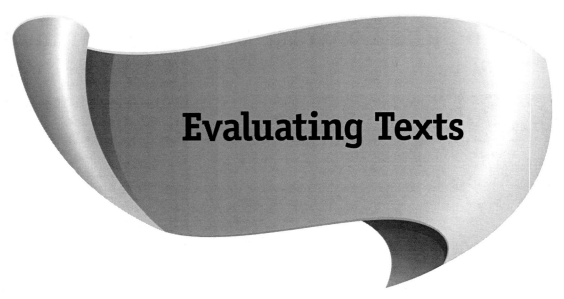

Evaluating Texts

Skill Overview

Students evaluate texts by conducting critical analyses of information and evidence in a text to make judgments about an idea, a course of action, or the outcomes of an event. Texts can also be evaluated to assess the strength of an author's claim, the strength of the author's evidence to support a claim, the criteria the author uses to identify evidence, and the overall development of the central message of a text.

Students often find it easy to make judgments or state their positions, whereas using textual evidence to support their judgments can prove more difficult. Requiring students to consistently use evidence from the text to justify their evaluations in writing and in class discussions ensures that students have frequent opportunities to apply this skill. This skill can be easily transferred to other content areas as students use evidence to support their claims and evaluations of other types of texts.

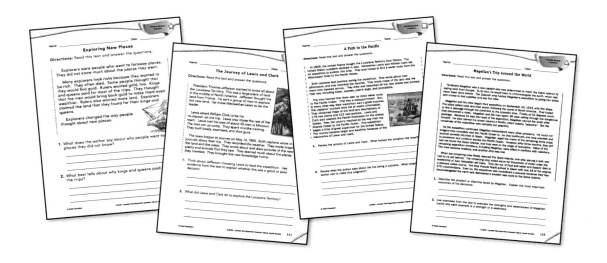

Implementing the Question Stems

This section includes 10 leveled, text-dependent question stems about evaluating texts. You can implement these question stems by connecting them to the texts that you are reading in class.

It may seem as though using question stems would be easy, but it can be a complex task for teachers. To help you see how to implement these question stems in your classroom, this section includes student pages containing texts with sample text-dependent questions. Each of the four student pages illustrates a different complexity level.

Snapshot of Differentiating a Question

The chart below models how a single leveled question stem can be tied to social studies texts at four complexity levels. This snapshot also gives a quick view of how the question stems differ based on the complexity levels. However, you can also see how the question stems link to one another.

	Question Stem	Example
☆	What did _____ (person) do to solve _____ (problem)?	What did Clara Barton do to help people?
○	Identify the problem faced by _____ (person). What was the outcome of his/her decision(s)?	Identify the problem faced by Helen Keller. What was the outcome of her decisions?
□	Describe the problem faced by _____ (person). What was the most important outcome of his/her decision(s)?	Describe the problem faced by Martin Luther King Jr. What was the most important outcome of his decisions?
△	Describe the problem or dilemma faced by _____ (person). Describe the most important outcomes of his/her decision(s).	Describe the problem or dilemma faced by James Madison in 1812. Describe the most important outcomes of his decisions.

Evaluating Texts Question Stems

Use these question stems to develop your own questions for students.

What best tells about _____ (*concept*)?

Does the text say something that you do not agree with? If so, why?

Think about _____ (*decision*). What would you have done differently?

What did _____ (*person*) do to solve _____ (*problem*)?

Do you agree with what _____ (*person*) did? Why or why not?

Who helped the most to _____ (*action*)? Why?

Who helped the least to _____ (*action*)? Why?

How did _____ (*person*) show strength?

Which text tells about _____ (*cause/argument*) better? Why?

What does the author say about _____ (*concept/event*)?

Name: _____   Date: _____

Exploring New Places

Directions: Read this text, and answer the questions.

Explorers were people who went to faraway places. They did not know much about the places they went. They often died on their trips. Still, many explorers took risks because they wanted to be rich. Some of them thought that they would find gold. Rulers wanted gold, too. Kings and queens paid for most of the trips. They thought that the men would bring back gold to make them even wealthier. Rulers also wanted more land. Explorers claimed the land that they found for their kings and queens.

Explorers changed the way people thought about new places.

1. What does the author say about why people went to places they did not know?

   _____

   _____

   _____

2. What best tells about why kings and queens paid for the trips?

   _____

   _____

   _____

Evaluating Texts Question Stems

Use these question stems to develop your own questions for students.

What evidence about _____ (*concept*) is the most convincing?

What evidence about _____ (*concept*) do you find unconvincing?

Think about _____ (*decision*). Use evidence from the text to explain whether this was a good or a poor decision.

Identify the problem faced by _____ (*person*). What was the outcome of his/her decision(s)?

Do you think _____ (*person*) chose the best course of action? Explain using details from the text.

What did _____ (*person/group*) do to _____ (*action*)?

Who helped the least to address _____ (*problem*)? Why?

Provide an example of a time _____ (*person*) showed strength. Why does this show strength?

Which text makes a stronger case for _____ (*cause/argument*)? Use evidence to justify your position.

Review what the author says about _____ (*concept/event*). Why does the author make this claim?

Name: _____ Date: _____

The Journey of Lewis and Clark

Directions: Read this text, and answer the questions.

President Thomas Jefferson wanted to know all about the Louisiana Territory. This was a large piece of land in the middle of North America. Jefferson bought the land from France. He sent a group of men to explore this new land. He chose Meriwether Lewis to be the leader.

Lewis asked William Clark to be his co-captain on the trip. Lewis also chose the rest of the team. Lewis met his crew of about 45 men in Missouri. The men set up camp. They spent months training. They built boats, exercised, and shot guns.

The team began its journey on May 14, 1804. Both captains wrote in journals about their trip. They recorded the weather. They made maps of the land and the water. They wrote about and drew pictures of the new plants and animals that they saw. They learned much about the places they traveled. They brought this new knowledge home.

1. Think about Jefferson choosing Lewis to lead the expedition. Use evidence from the text to explain whether this was a good or poor decision.

_____

_____

2. What did Lewis and Clark do to explore the Louisiana Territory?

_____

_____

_____

Evaluating Texts Question Stems

Use these question stems to develop your own questions for students.

Review all the evidence for _____ (*concept*). What evidence do you find most convincing and why?

What evidence about the author's point on _____ (*concept*) do you find unconvincing? Why is it unconvincing?

Review _____ (*decision*) made by _____ (*person/group*). How might this decision be improved upon or strengthened?

Describe the problem faced by _____ (*person*). What was the most important outcome of his/her decision(s)?

Analyze whether _____ (*person*) made the best decision(s) to solve _____ (*problem*). Use details from the text to explain your position.

Review the actions of _____ (*person/group*). What helped the situation the most? How?

Which action taken by _____ (*person/group*) was least effective in addressing _____ (*problem*)? Why?

Use examples from the text to describe the strengths and weaknesses of _____ (*person/group*).

Analyze the evidence in both texts that support _____ (*cause/argument*). Use the texts to explain which author makes a stronger case.

Review what the author says about _____ (*concept/event*). What criteria does the author use to make this judgment?

Name: _____ Date: _____

A Path to the Pacific

Directions: Read this text, and answer the questions.

In 1803, the United States bought the Louisiana Territory from France. The United States suddenly doubled in size. Meriwether Lewis and William Clark led an expedition to explore this area. They also hoped to find a water route from the Mississippi River to the Pacific Ocean.

Both captains kept journals during the expedition. They wrote about their adventures, and they recorded the weather. They made maps of the land and the rivers they traveled across. They drew and described all the new plants and animals they saw, including bison, coyotes, prairie dogs, and jackrabbits.

The men learned that there was no direct water route to the Pacific Ocean. That was a disappointment. But, in every other way, their expedition was a great success. The captains' journals were full of useful information. They contained maps of the land and descriptions of 178 new plants and 122 new animals. Lewis and Clark also claimed the Pacific Northwest for the United States. Now, the country reached all the way from the Atlantic Ocean to the Pacific Ocean. This expedition began a time of great expansion for the United States. The country became larger and wealthier because of the discoveries of Lewis and Clark.

1. Review the actions of Lewis and Clark. What helped the situation the most? How?

   _____

   _____

   _____

2. Review what the author says about the trip being a success. What criteria does the author use to make this judgment?

   _____

   _____

   _____

COMPLEXITY

Evaluating Texts Question Stems

Use these question stems to develop your own questions for students.

Determine the most convincing evidence the author provides to show _____ (*concept*). Explain why you think this evidence is the most convincing.

Identify any unconvincing evidence the author provides to support his/her argument about _____ (*concept*). Explain why you find it unconvincing.

Review the outcome of _____ (*decision*) made by _____ (*person/group*). Use the text to determine how this decision could have been improved or strengthened.

Describe the problem or dilemma faced by _____ (*person*). Explain the most important outcomes of his/her decision(s).

Evaluate whether the decision(s) made by _____ (*person*) was/were the best solution(s) to solve _____ (*problem*). Use evidence from the text to justify your position.

Analyze the actions taken by _____ (*person/group*) in response to _____ (*event*). Use evidence from the text to explain which was the best course of action.

Analyze the actions taken by _____ (*person*) in response to _____ (*event*). Use evidence from the text to explain which was the least effective course of action.

Use examples from the text to evaluate the strengths and weaknesses of _____ (*person/group*). Justify why each example is a strength or a weakness.

Analyze the evidence in both texts that support _____ (*cause/ argument*). Use the texts to explain which author makes a stronger case and what specific evidence better supports his/ her case.

Analyze the author's evaluation of _____ (*concept/event*). Determine what criteria the author uses to make this judgment.

Name: _____ Date: _____

Magellan's Trip Around the World

Directions: Read this text, and answer the questions.

Ferdinand Magellan was a sea captain who was determined to reach the Spice Islands by sailing west from Europe. To do this, he would have to circumnavigate the earth, which had never been done before. The Spanish king funded Magellan's expedition by giving him ships and money to buy supplies and pay the crew.

Magellan and his crew began their expedition on September 20, 1519, with five ships. The ships sailed west and then south, following the coast of South America. They hoped to find a passage through the continent to the opposite side. Finally, at 52 degrees south, they discovered a strait. Magellan and his men spent 38 days sailing through the dangerous passage. Because he was the head of the expedition, Magellan named the strait after himself. He also named the ocean beyond it Pacific, which means "peaceful." But the remainder of the expedition was certainly not peaceful.

As the expedition continued, Magellan encountered many other problems. He could not imagine how incredibly vast the Pacific Ocean is. As they continued, one ship wrecked and another secretly returned to Spain. Magellan urged the crews of the remaining three ships to persevere and continue across the Pacific Ocean. However, after three months, they still had not found the Spice Islands, and they were on the verge of starvation. Many of the remaining expedition members, including Magellan, were killed in conflicts with islanders. The crew became restless, and another ship was lost.

When the remaining crew finally reached the Spice Islands, one ship sprung a leak and had to be left behind. The remaining ship sailed alone for thousands of miles under the leadership of Juan Sebastián del Cano. They ran out of food and water, and dozens died of a disease called scurvy. The ship *Victoria* finally arrived in Spain with only 18 of the original 270 crewmembers. Even so, the expedition was considered a success because they had circumnavigated the earth and discovered a western sea route to the Spice Islands.

1. Describe the problem or dilemma faced by Magellan. Explain the most important outcomes of his decisions.

   _____

   _____

2. Use examples from the text to evaluate the strengths and weaknesses of Magellan. Justify why each example is a strength or a weakness.

   _____

   _____

Evaluating Texts K–12 Alignment

Use this chart to determine the best question stems for your different groups of students.

★	●	■	▲
What best tells about _____ (concept)?	What evidence about _____ (concept) is the most convincing?	Review all the evidence for _____ (concept). What evidence do you find most convincing and why?	Determine the most convincing evidence the author provides to show _____ (concept). Explain why you think this evidence is the most convincing.
Does the text say something that you do not agree with? If so, why?	What evidence about _____ (concept) do you find unconvincing?	What evidence about the author's point on _____ (concept) do you find unconvincing? Why is it unconvincing?	Identify any unconvincing evidence the author provides to support his/her argument about _____ (concept). Explain why you find it unconvincing.
Think about _____ (decision). What would you have done differently?	Think about _____ (decision). Use evidence from the text to explain whether this was a good or a poor decision.	Review _____ (decision) made by _____ (person/group). How might this decision be improved upon or strengthened?	Review the outcome of _____ (decision) made by _____ (person/group). Use the text to determine how this decision could have been improved or strengthened.
What did _____ (person) do to solve _____ (problem)?	Identify the problem faced by _____ (person). What was the outcome of his/her decision(s)?	Describe the problem faced by _____ (person). What was the most important outcome of his/her decision(s)?	Describe the problem or dilemma faced by _____ (person). Explain the most important outcomes of his/her decision(s).
Do you agree with what _____ (person) did? Why or why not?	Do you think _____ (person) chose the best course of action? Explain using details from the text.	Analyze whether _____ (person) made the best decision(s) to solve _____ (problem). Use details from the text to explain your position.	Evaluate whether the decision(s) made by _____ (person) was/were the best solution(s) to solve _____ (problem). Use evidence from the text to justify your position.

Evaluating Texts K–12 Alignment *(cont.)*

★	●	■	▲
Who helped the most to _____ (*action*)? Why?	What did _____ (*person/group*) do to _____ (*action*)?	Review the actions of _____ (*person/group*). What helped the situation the most? How?	Analyze the actions taken by _____ (*person/group*) in response to _____ (*event*). Use evidence from the text to explain which was the best course of action.
Who helped the least to _____ (*action*)? Why?	Who helped the least to address _____ (*problem*)? Why?	Which action taken by _____ (*person/group*) was least effective in addressing _____ (*problem*)? Why?	Analyze the actions taken by _____ (*person*) in response to _____ (*event*). Use evidence from the text to explain which was the least effective course of action.
How did _____ (*person*) show strength?	Provide an example of a time _____ (*person*) showed strength. Why does this show strength?	Use examples from the text to describe the strengths and weaknesses of _____ (*person/group*).	Use examples from the text to evaluate the strengths and weaknesses of _____ (*person/ group*). Justify why each example is a strength or a weakness.
Which text tells about _____ (*cause/argument*) better? Why?	Which text makes a stronger case for _____ (*cause/ argument*)? Use evidence to justify your position.	Analyze the evidence in both texts that support _____ (*cause/argument*). Use the texts to explain which author makes a stronger case.	Analyze the evidence in both texts that support _____ (*cause/argument*). Use the texts to explain which author makes a stronger case and what specific evidence better supports his/her case.
What does the author say about _____ (*concept/ event*)?	Review what the author says about _____ (*concept/ event*). Why does the author make this claim?	Review what the author says about _____ (*concept/ event*). What criteria does the author use to make this judgment?	Analyze the author's evaluation of _____ (*concept/event*). Determine what criteria the author uses to make this judgment.

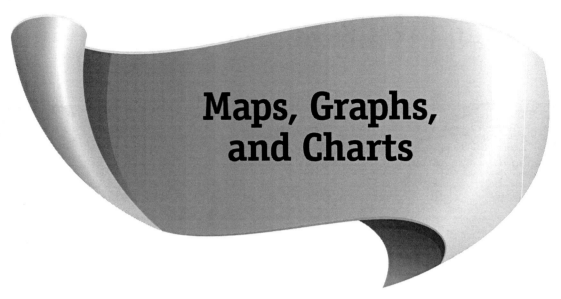

Maps, Graphs, and Charts

Skill Overview

The ability to understand and analyze maps, graphs, and charts is a fundamental skill for social studies students. Analyzing the features of these items allows students to identify patterns in information presented through various formats.

Maps, graphs, and charts can enhance a secondary-source text and help students better understand what they are reading. But maps, graphs, and charts can be primary sources themselves. As primary sources, they serve as windows into the past or present. Through analysis and interpretation, students can discover what the creators of these primary sources thought was important, the trends and relationships the creators saw, and how people saw the world at the time. Incorporating maps, graphs, and charts into text analysis deepens students' comprehension of people, places, events, and concepts.

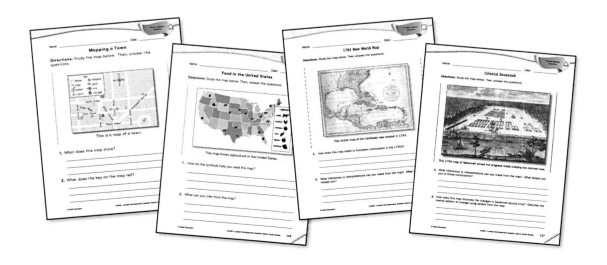

Implementing the Question Stems

This section includes 10 leveled, text-dependent question stems about maps, graphs, and charts. You can implement these question stems by connecting them to the texts that you are reading in class.

It may seem as though using question stems would be easy, but it can be a complex task for teachers. To help you see how to implement these question stems in your classroom, this section includes student pages containing texts with sample text-dependent questions. Each of the four student pages illustrates a different complexity level.

Snapshot of Differentiating a Question

The chart below models how a single leveled question stem can be tied to social studies texts at four complexity levels. This snapshot also gives a quick view of how the question stems differ based on the complexity levels. However, you can also see how the question stems link to one another.

	Question Stem	Example
☆	What does this map/graph/chart tell about _____ (*person/place/event/time period/concept*)?	What does this chart tell about people who help?
○	How does this map/graph/chart help you understand _____ (*person/place/event/time period/concept*)?	How does this map help you understand your city?
▢	How does this map/graph/chart relate to _____ (*person/place/event/time period/concept*)?	How does this map relate to the Age of Exploration?
△	Describe the relationship between the map/graph/chart and _____ (*person/place/event/time period/concept*).	Describe the relationship between the chart and the unemployment rate in the United States.

Maps, Graphs, and Charts Question Stems

Use these question stems to develop your own questions for students.

What does the _____ (*feature*) on the map/graph/chart tell?

How does the map/graph/chart use symbols/colors?

How does the map/graph/chart help you understand _____ (*concept*)?

What does this map/graph/chart tell about _____ (*person/place/event/time period/concept*)?

What can you learn from the map/graph/chart that is not stated?

What is different about the two maps?

What does this map show?

What does the graph show?

How is the chart organized?

Why is the map/graph/chart important?

Name: _____ Date: _____

Mapping a Town

Directions: Study the map below. Then, answer
the questions.

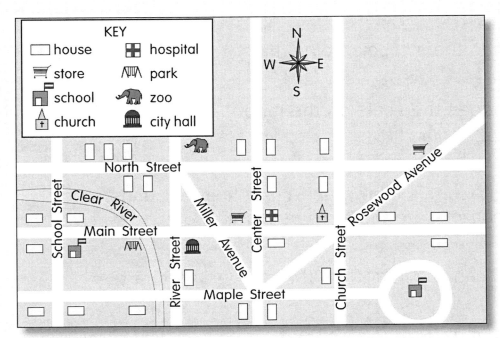

This is a map of a town.

1. What does this map show?

_____

_____

_____

2. What does the key on the map tell?

_____

_____

_____

Maps, Graphs, and Charts Question Stems

Use these question stems to develop your own questions for students.

What kind of information does the _____ (*feature*) on the map/graph/chart show?

How do the symbols/colors help you read the map/graph/chart?

How does the scale on the map/graph/chart help you understand _____ (*concept*)?

How does this map/graph/chart help you understand _____ (*person/place/event/time period/concept*)?

What can you infer from the map/graph/chart?

What is different about the two maps? Why is there a difference?

How does this map show changes in _____ (*location*)?

What overall trend is shown in the graph?

Why is the chart organized by _____ (*organization*)?

Where does the information in the map/graph/chart come from? Why is it important?

Name: _____ Date: _____

Food in the United States

Directions: Study the map below. Then, answer the questions.

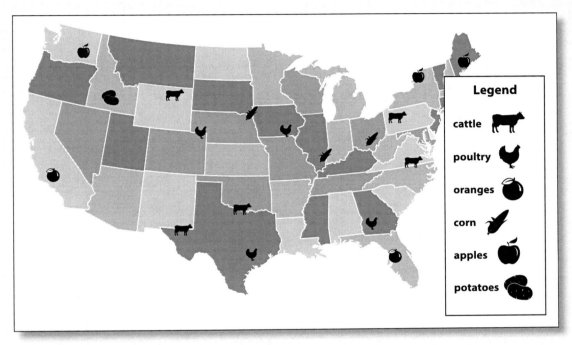

This map shows agriculture in the United States.

1. How do the symbols help you read the map?

    _____

    _____

    _____

2. What can you infer from the map?

    _____

    _____

    _____

Maps, Graphs, and Charts Question Stems

Use these question stems to develop your own questions for students.

What kind of information does the _____ (*feature*) on the map/graph/chart contain? Why is this information useful?

- -

What does each symbol/color on the map/graph/chart mean? How does each help you understand the map/graph/chart?

- -

How can you tell whether the scale on the map/graph/chart accurately represents _____ (*concept*)?

- -

How does this map/graph/chart relate to _____ (*person/ place/event/time period/concept*)?

- -

What inferences or interpretations can you make from the map/ graph/chart? What details helped you?

- -

Study a political map of _____ (*location*) before and after _____ (*event*). Describe how the boundaries have changed.

- -

How does this map illustrate the changes in _____ (*location*) across time?

- -

What conclusions can you draw based on the overall trend in the graph?

- -

How is the chart organized? How does that make it easier to understand?

- -

Where does the information in the map/graph/chart come from? Why did the author think it was important?

Name: _____ Date: _____

1783 New World Map

Directions: Study the map below. Then, answer the questions.

This British map of the Caribbean was created in 1783.

1. How does this map relate to European colonization in the 1700s?

_____

_____

_____

2. What inferences or interpretations can you make from the map? What details helped you?

_____

_____

_____

COMPLEXITY

LOW  HIGH

Maps, Graphs, and Charts Question Stems

Use these question stems to develop your own questions for students.

What type of information is displayed in the _____ (*feature*) of the map/graph/chart? Explain why this information is important.

Describe how the symbols/colors help the reader interpret the map/graph/chart.

Analyze whether the scale on the map/graph/chart accurately represents _____ (*concept*). Use details from the text to support your claim.

Describe the relationship between the map/graph/chart and _____ (*person/place/event/time period/concept*).

What inferences or interpretations can you make from the map/graph/chart? What details led you to those conclusions?

Study a political map of _____ (*location*) before and after _____ (*event*). How have the boundaries changed? What were the causes and effects of these changes?

How does this map illustrate the changes in _____ (*location*) across time? Describe the overall pattern of change, using details from the map.

What does the overall trend in the graph tell us about the relationship between what is represented on the *x*-axis and the *y*-axis?

Describe how the chart is organized and how that makes it easier for the reader to understand.

What is the source of the information used in the map/graph/chart? Why did the author think it was important to include?

Name: _____ Date: _____

Colonial Savannah

Directions: Study the map below. Then, answer the questions.

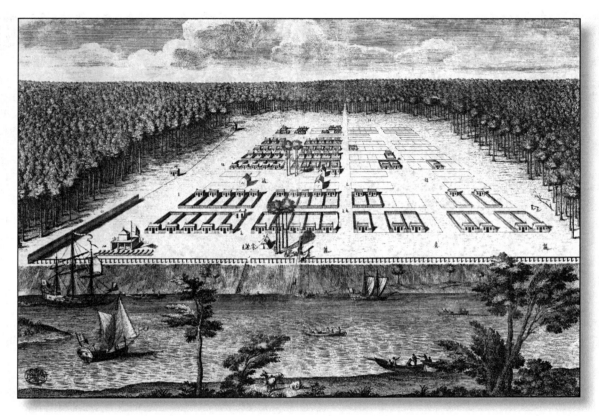

This 1734 map of Savannah shows the progress made building the colonial town.

1. What inferences or interpretations can you make from the map? What details led you to those conclusions?

   _____

   _____

   _____

2. How does this map illustrate the changes in Savannah across time? Describe the overall pattern of change, using details from the map.

   _____

   _____

   _____

Maps, Graphs, and Charts K–12 Alignment

Use this chart to determine the best question stems for your different groups of students.

★	●	■	▲
What does the _____ (feature) on the map/graph/chart tell?	What kind of information does the _____ (feature) on the map/graph/chart show?	What kind of information does the _____ (feature) on the map/graph/chart contain? Why is this information useful?	What type of information is displayed in the _____ (feature) of the map/graph/chart? Explain why this information is important.
How does the map/graph/chart use symbols/colors?	How do the symbols/colors help you read the map/graph/chart?	What does each symbol/color on the map/graph/chart mean? How does each help you understand the map/graph/chart?	Describe how the symbols/colors help the reader interpret the map/graph/chart.
How does the map/graph/chart help you understand _____ (concept)?	How does the scale on the map/graph/chart help you understand _____ (concept)?	How can you tell whether the scale on the map/graph/chart accurately represents _____ (concept)?	Analyze whether the scale on the map/graph/chart accurately represents _____ (concept). Use details from the text to support your claim.
What does this map/graph/chart tell about _____ (person/place/event/time period/concept)?	How does this map/graph/chart help you understand _____ (person/place/event/time period/concept)?	How does this map/graph/chart relate to _____ (person/place/event/time period/concept)?	Describe the relationship between the map/graph/chart and _____ (person/place/event/time period/concept).
What can you learn from the map/graph/chart that is not stated?	What can you infer from the map/graph/chart?	What inferences or interpretations can you make from the map/graph/chart? What details helped you?	What inferences or interpretations can you make from the map/graph/chart? What details led you to those conclusions?

Maps, Graphs, and Charts K–12 Alignment (cont.)

★	●	■	▲
What is different about the two maps?	What is different about the two maps? Why is there a difference?	Study a political map of _____ (location) before and after _____ (event). Describe how the boundaries have changed.	Study a political map of _____ (location) before and after _____ (event). How have the boundaries changed? What were the causes and effects of these changes?
What does this map show?	How does this map show changes in _____ (location)?	How does this map illustrate the changes in _____ (location) across time?	How does this map illustrate the changes in _____ (location) across time? Describe the overall pattern of change, using details from the map.
What does the graph show?	What overall trend is shown in the graph?	What conclusions can you draw based on the overall trend in the graph?	What does the overall trend in the graph tell us about the relationship between what is represented on the x-axis and the y-axis?
How is the chart organized?	Why is the chart organized by _____ (organization)?	How is the chart organized? How does that make it easier to understand?	Describe how the chart is organized and how that makes it easier for the reader to understand.
Why is the map/ graph/chart important?	Where does the information in the map/graph/chart come from? Why is it important?	Where does the information in the map/graph/chart come from? Why did the author think it was important?	What is the source of the information used in the map/graph/chart? Why did the author think it was important to include?

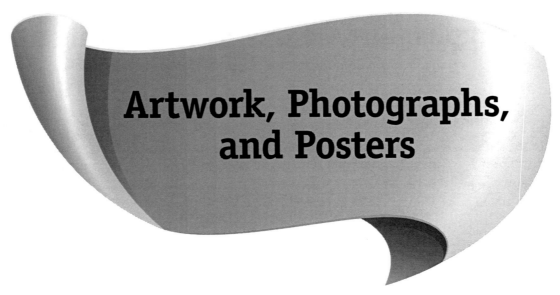

Artwork, Photographs, and Posters

Skill Overview

Studying social studies texts includes a variety of visual media. Artwork (including political cartoons), photographs, and posters are among the myriad of history/social studies sources. These visual media offer students the unique opportunity to both interpret the visuals and analyze the history behind them. Throughout time, artists have used visual media to raise awareness, express emotion, and capture moments in time. Visual media can show civil unrest, daily life, societal values, and how an artist sees his or her world. Students may study a single piece of art several times throughout a unit of study and learn something new from it each time as they continue to deepen their knowledge of the history behind it.

Artwork, photographs, and posters can be treated as complex text. The same social studies literacy skills applied to other forms of text can also be applied to the analysis of these visual media. These skills include interpreting content, analyzing perspectives, making inferences, and comparing and contrasting.

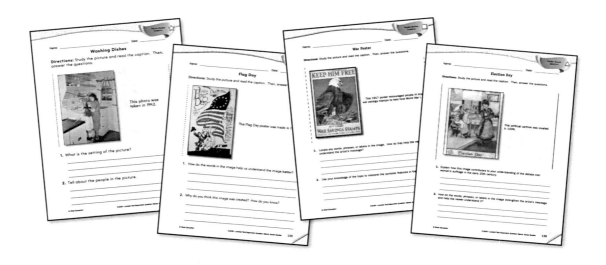

Implementing the Question Stems

This section includes 10 leveled, text-dependent question stems about artwork, photographs, and posters. You can implement these question stems by connecting them to the texts that you are reading in class.

It may seem as though using question stems would be easy, but it can be a complex task for teachers. To help you see how to implement these question stems in your classroom, this section includes student pages containing texts with sample text-dependent questions. Each of the four student pages illustrates a different complexity level.

Snapshot of Differentiating a Question

The chart below models how a single leveled question stem can be tied to social studies texts at four complexity levels. This snapshot also gives a quick view of how the question stems differ based on the complexity levels. However, you can also see how the question stems link to one another.

	Question Stem	Example
☆	What does this picture tell you about _____ (person/place/event/time period)?	What does this picture tell you about being a good leader?
○	How does this image help you better understand _____ (person/place/event/time period)?	How does this image help you better understand American Indians?
□	How does this image contribute to your understanding of _____ (person/place/event/time period)?	How does this image contribute to your understanding of daily life in Mesopotamia?
△	Explain how this image contributes to your understanding of _____ (person/place/event/time period).	Explain how this image contributes to your understanding of postwar Europe.

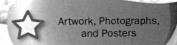

Artwork, Photographs, and Posters Question Stems

Use these question stems to develop your own questions for students.

Describe the colors used in the picture.

Tell about the people in the picture.

What is the setting of the picture?

What is the title of the picture?

What else should the artist have shown in the picture?

What do the words/phrases/labels say? Why are they in the picture?

When was this picture made?

Why do you think this picture was made?

What does this picture tell you about _____ (*person/place/ event/time period*)?

Are there any symbols in the picture? What do they mean/ stand for?

Name: _____ Date: _____

Washing Dishes

Directions: Study the picture, and read the caption. Then, answer the questions.

This photo was taken in 1942.

1. What is the setting of the picture?

_____

_____

_____

2. Tell about the people in the picture.

_____

_____

_____

Artwork, Photographs, and Posters Question Stems

Use these question stems to develop your own questions for students.

How do the colors help us understand the image?

Describe the people in the image.

Describe the setting of the image.

What do you learn from the title of the image?

Is anything missing from the image that the artist should have included?

How do the words/phrases/labels in the image help us understand the image better?

When was the image made? How is the image related to that time?

Why was this image created? How do you know?

How does this image help you better understand _____ (*person/place/event/time period*)?

Describe the symbols included in the image.

Name: _____ Date: _____

Flag Day

Directions: Study the picture, and read the caption. Then, answer the questions.

This Flag Day poster was made in 1917.

1. How do the words in the image help us understand the image better?

   _____

   _____

   _____

2. Why do you think this image was created? How do you know?

   _____

   _____

   _____

Artwork, Photographs, and Posters Question Stems

Use these question stems to develop your own questions for students.

What do the colors tell us about what the artist is trying to communicate?

Describe the people in the image. What strikes you about their expressions/actions/postures?

Describe the setting of the image. Why is that important?

What does the title clarify about the image?

Based on what you know about _____ (*event/time period/ concept*), should anything else be included in the image?

Locate any words, phrases, or labels in the image. How do they help the viewer understand the artist's message?

When was the image created? How does the image relate to the time period in which it was created?

What can you infer about why the image was created? Use evidence from the image and what you know about the time period to support your claim.

How does this image contribute to your understanding of _____ (*person/place/event/time period*)?

Use your knowledge of the time period/topic to interpret the symbolic features in the image.

Name: _____ Date: _____

War Poster

Directions: Study the picture, and read the caption. Then, answer the questions.

This 1917 poster encouraged people to buy war savings stamps to help fund World War I.

1. Locate any words, phrases, or labels in the image. How do they help the viewer understand the artist's message?

    _____

    _____

    _____

2. Use your knowledge of the topic to interpret the symbolic features in the image.

    _____

    _____

    _____

COMPLEXITY

LOW  HIGH

Artwork, Photographs, and Posters Question Stems

Use these question stems to develop your own questions for students.

Describe how the colors in the image help the viewer understand the artist's message.

Describe the people in the image. What can you infer from their expressions/actions/postures?

Describe the setting of the image and how it relates to _____ (*event/time period/concept*).

What does the title of the image reveal about the artist's message?

Based on what you know about _____ (*event/time period/ concept*), is there anything else that should be included in the image? Explain why you think the image is complete or what you think is missing and why.

How do the words, phrases, or labels in the image strengthen the artist's message and help the viewer understand it?

What is the author's purpose in creating this image? How is it related to the time period in which it was created?

What can you infer about why the image was created? Use evidence from the image and what you know about the artist and the historical context of the image to support your claim.

Explain how this image contributes to your understanding of _____ (*person/place/event/time period*).

Use your knowledge of the time period/topic to interpret the symbolic features in the image. Why do you think the artist chose these symbols?

Name: _____ Date: _____

Election Day

Directions: Study the picture, and read the caption. Then, answer the questions.

This political cartoon was created in 1909.

1. Explain how this image contributes to your understanding of the debate over women's suffrage in the early 20th century.

   _____

   _____

   _____

2. How do the words, phrases, or labels in the image strengthen the artist's message and help the viewer understand it?

   _____

   _____

   _____

Artwork, Photographs, and Posters
K–12 Alignment

Use this chart to determine the best question stems for your different groups of students.

★	●	■	▲
Describe the colors used in the picture.	How do the colors help us understand the image?	What do the colors tell us about what the artist is trying to communicate?	Describe how the colors in the image help the viewer understand the artist's message.
Tell about the people in the picture.	Describe the people in the image.	Describe the people in the image. What strikes you about their expressions/actions/postures?	Describe the people in the image. What can you infer from their expressions/actions/postures?
What is the setting of the picture?	Describe the setting of the image.	Describe the setting of the image. Why is that important?	Describe the setting of the image and how it relates to _____ (event/time period/concept).
What is the title of the picture?	What do you learn from the title of the image?	What does the title clarify about the image?	What does the title of the image reveal about the artist's message?
What else should the artist have shown in the picture?	Is anything missing from the image that the artist should have included?	Based on what you know about _____ (event/time period/concept), should anything else be included in the image?	Based on what you know about _____ (event/time period/concept), is there anything else that should be included in the image? Explain why you think the image is complete or what you think is missing and why.

Artwork, Photographs, and Posters
K–12 Alignment (cont.)

★	●	■	▲
What do the words/phrases/labels say? Why are they in the picture?	How do the words/phrases/labels in the image help us understand the image better?	Locate any words, phrases, or labels in the image. How do they help the viewer understand the artist's message?	How do the words, phrases, or labels in the image strengthen the artist's message and help the viewer understand it?
When was this picture made?	When was the image made? How is the image related to that time?	When was the image created? How does the image relate to the time period in which it was created?	What is the author's purpose in creating this image? How is it related to the time period in which it was created?
Why do you think this picture was made?	Why was this image created? How do you know?	What can you infer about why the image was created? Use evidence from the image and what you know about the time period to support your claim.	What can you infer about why the image was created? Use evidence from the image and what you know about the artist and the historical context of the image to support your claim.
What does this picture tell you about _____ (person/place/event/time period)?	How does this image help you better understand _____ (person/place/event/time period)?	How does this image contribute to your understanding of _____ (person/place/event/time period)?	Explain how this image contributes to your understanding of _____ (person/place/event/time period).
Are there any symbols in the picture? What do they mean/stand for?	Describe the symbols included in the image.	Use your knowledge of the time period/topic to interpret the symbolic features in the image.	Use your knowledge of the time period/topic to interpret the symbolic features in the image. Why do you think the artist chose these symbols?

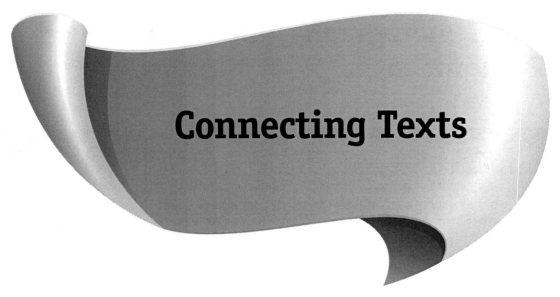

Connecting Texts

Skill Overview

Connecting texts is one of the highest levels of analysis students can undertake. Establishing connections between texts requires the application of several social studies skills, including summarizing positions, determining cause and effect, analyzing multiple perspectives, and comparing and contrasting. In many ways, this skill is a culmination of many other key social studies skills.

For students who are just beginning to connect multiple texts, sufficient practice is needed before additional texts can be introduced. As students' abilities to analyze multiple texts improve, teachers can increase the variety and complexity of texts used. As students become more experienced with this skill, they will begin to see texts through more analytical lenses. They will learn to not only make connections between the content of the texts but also between the perspectives, points of view, opinions, text structures, and purposes of various texts. This can also be a great way for students to analyze the differences between primary and secondary sources on the same topics.

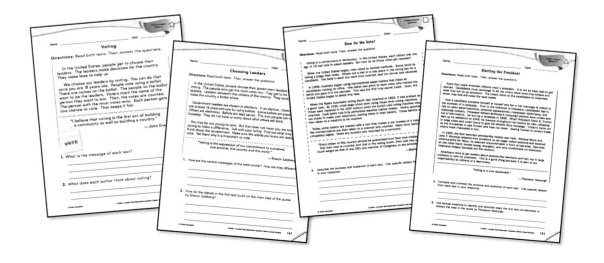

Implementing the Question Stems

This section includes 10 leveled, text-dependent question stems about connecting texts. You can implement these question stems by connecting them to the texts that you are reading in class. **Note:** Each activity sheet in this section uses a short passage and a quotation for text comparison. However, the question stems are written for a variety of text types.

It may seem as though using question stems would be easy, but it can be a complex task for teachers. To help you see how to implement these question stems in your classroom, this section includes student pages containing texts with sample text-dependent questions. Each of the four student pages illustrates a different complexity level.

Snapshot of Differentiating a Question

The chart below models how a single leveled question stem can be tied to social studies texts at four complexity levels. This snapshot also gives a quick view of how the question stems differ based on the complexity levels. However, you can also see how the question stems link to one another.

	Question Stem	Example
☆	Think about how each author tells about _____ (*event/concept*). How are they different?	Think about how each author tells about rules. How are they different?
○	Reread how each author describes _____ (*event/concept*). List ways in which their descriptions are different.	Reread how each author describes Columbus's voyage. List ways in which their descriptions are different.
▢	Analyze the retelling of _____ (*event/concept*) by each author. Describe the points that conflict with each other.	Analyze the retelling of civic duty by each author. Describe the points that conflict with each other.
△	Analyze the retelling of _____ (*event/concept*) presented by each author. Explain where the accounts conflict with each other.	Analyze the retelling of the building of the Great Wall of China presented by each author. Explain where the accounts conflict with each other.

COMPLEXITY

LOW   HIGH

Connecting Texts Question Stems

Use these question stems to develop your own questions for students.

Why was each text written?

What is the message of each text?

How do the authors of the texts agree? How do they disagree?

What does _____ (text A) tell about? What does _____ (text B) tell about?

_____ (text B) tells about _____ (problem). How is it solved in _____ (text A)?

How are the ideas in _____ (text A) and _____ (text B) the same? How are they different?

What details in _____ (text A) tell more about _____ (main idea in text B)?

What does each author think about _____ (event/concept)?

Think about how each author tells about _____ (event/concept). How are they different?

Do the texts have the same purpose/point of view? How do you know?

Name: _____ Date: _____

Voting

Directions: Read both texts. Then, answer the questions.

In the United States, people get to choose their leaders. The leaders make decisions for the country. They make laws to help people.

Americans choose leaders by voting. They can do that once they are 18 years old. People vote using a ballot. There are names on the ballot. The people on the ballot want to be the leaders. Voters mark the name of the person they want to win. Then, the votes are counted. The person with the most votes wins. Each person gets one chance to vote. That keeps it fair.

"I believe that voting is the first act of building a community as well as building a country."

—John Ensign

1. What is the message of each text?

_____

_____

_____

2. What does each author think about voting?

_____

_____

Connecting Texts Question Stems

Use these question stems to develop your own questions for students.

For whom was each text written? Why?

How are the central messages of the texts similar? How are they different?

On which points do the authors of the texts agree? On which points do they disagree?

How does _____ (text A) describe what happens in _____ (text B)?

What solutions can be found in _____ (text A) to support the problem described in _____ (text B)?

In what ways do _____ (text A) and _____ (text B) describe the same ideas? In what ways do they describe different ideas?

How do details in _____ (text A) build on the main ideas in _____ (text B)?

What is each author's opinion about _____ (event/concept)? How does this affect their descriptions?

Reread how each author describes _____ (event/concept). List ways in which their descriptions are different.

Describe how the texts have the same purpose/point of view/ text structure.

Name: _____ Date: _____

Choosing Leaders

Directions: Read both texts. Then, answer the questions.

In the United States, people choose their government leaders by voting. The people who get the most votes win. They get to be the leaders. Leaders represent the citizens of the country. They work to make the country a better place.

Government leaders are chosen in elections. In an election, citizens who are at least 18 years old vote using ballots. Some ballots are paper. Others are electronic. Ballots are kept secret. This is so people can vote honestly. They do not have to worry about what others will think.

You may be too young to vote. But that does not mean you are too young to make a difference. Talk with your family. Find out what they think about the government. Make sure the adults you know are ready to vote. Tell them why it is important to vote.

"Voting is the expression of our commitment to ourselves,
one another, this country and this world."

—Sharon Salzberg

1. How are the central messages of the texts similar? How are they different?

_____

_____

_____

2. How do the details in the first text build on the main idea of the quote by Sharon Salzberg?

_____

_____

_____

Connecting Texts Question Stems

Use these question stems to develop your own questions for students.

Describe the purpose and audience of each text. Cite specific details from the text in your response.

- -

Compare and contrast the central messages of the texts.

- -

Cite specific points where the authors agree and where the authors disagree.

- -

How does _____ (text A) describe a cause? How does _____ (text B) describe the outcome/effect? Use evidence from the text to support your ideas.

- -

Cite the solution(s) found in _____ (text A) for the problem(s) described in _____ (text B).

- -

Identify how _____ (text A) corroborates or refutes the idea(s) in _____ (text B). Use the texts to support your answer.

- -

Use textual evidence to show how details in _____ (text A) elaborate upon the main ideas in _____ (text B).

- -

Explain how each author's perspective influences how the events are described in each text.

- -

Analyze the retelling of _____ (event/concept) by each author. Describe the points that conflict with each other.

- -

How could the texts be grouped based on purpose/point of view/text structure?

Name: _____ Date: _____

How Do We Vote?

Directions: Read both texts. Then, answer the question.

Voting is a cornerstone of democracy. In the United States, each citizen over the age of 18 can vote to select leaders. But how do all those votes get counted?

When the United States began, men voted by several methods. Some voted by telling a judge their votes. Others put a ball or a clay piece in the voting box for a candidate. The balls in each box were then counted, and the winner was declared.

In 1858, Australia began using standardized paper ballots that listed all candidates running for office. One ballot was given to each voter, who marked his ballot and gave it to the recorder. This was the first truly secret ballot. Soon, the United States began to adopt this idea.

When the Myers Automatic Voting Booth was invented in 1892, it was praised as a great idea. By 1930, most large cities were using these lever voting machines. These were replaced in the 20th century when the punch card voting machine was invented. Each ballot had little perforated squares (called chads). Voters punched out chads to make their selections, leaving holes in their ballots. These ballots were then taken to a machine to be counted.

Today, some ballots are marked with a tool that makes a dot instead of a hole. The marked ballots are then taken to a scanner and counted. Many other ballots are completely digital. Votes are counted and recorded by a computer.

- -

"Every citizen of this country should be guaranteed that their vote matters, that their vote is counted, and that in the voting booth, their vote has as much weight as that of any CEO, any member of Congress, or any president."

—Barbara Boxer

1. Describe the purpose and audience of each text. Cite specific details from the text in your response.

_____

_____

_____

_____

Connecting Texts Question Stems

Use these question stems to develop your own questions for students.

Compare and contrast the purpose and audience of each text. Cite specific details from each text in your response.

Compare and contrast the central messages of the texts. Explain how the central messages agree or conflict with each other.

Cite specific points in the texts where the authors agree and where they disagree. Use evidence from the texts to explain why they agree and disagree.

Use textual evidence to explain how _____ (text A) describes the cause of an outcome/effect described in _____ (text B).

Use textual evidence to explain how _____ (text A) provides solution(s) to the problem(s) described in _____ (text B).

Use textual evidence to describe ways in which _____ (text A) corroborates or refutes the idea(s) in _____ (text B).

Identify textual evidence to explain how details in _____ (text A) elaborate upon the main ideas in _____ (text B).

Describe how the perspectives of each author are similar and different. Explain how this influences the ideas presented in each text.

Analyze the retelling of _____ (event/concept) presented by each author. Explain where the accounts conflict with each other.

Describe how the texts can be categorized based on purpose/ point of view/text structure.

Name: _____ Date: _____

Electing the President

Directions: Read both texts. Then, answer the questions.

Every four years, American citizens elect a president. It is not an easy task to get elected. Candidates must campaign to let the voters know what they believe and what they will do as president. The voters listen to the candidates to determine whom they feel will make the best leader.

How a candidate presents himself or herself and his or her message is critical to the success of a campaign. Prior to the invention of television, candidates had to rely on radio advertisements, personal appearances, newspaper advertising, and elaborate posters. President William McKinley's campaign posters were ornate and full of information. He won by a landslide in 1896. When President Harry S. Truman was up for reelection in 1948, he traveled throughout the country by train, stopping in large cities and small towns to give his Whistle Stop message. Citizens came out by the thousands to see Truman and hear his views. Seeing Truman in person made voters more interested in him.

In 1960, the first televised presidential debate was held. Richard Nixon and John F. Kennedy debated their positions as an eager nation watched and listened. Unfortunately for Nixon, he seemed uncomfortable in front of cameras. Kennedy, on the other hand, looked young, energetic, and very comfortable on television. Television helped Kennedy win the election.

Americans tend to get excited about presidential elections and turn out in large numbers to vote for president. This is a good thing because it is part of our responsibility as citizens of a democracy.

"Voting is a civic sacrament."

—Theodore Hesburgh

1. Compare and contrast the purpose and audience of each text. Cite specific details from each text in your response.

   _____

   _____

2. Use textual evidence to describe ways in which the first text corroborates or refutes the idea in the quote by Theodore Hesburgh.

   _____

   _____

Connecting Texts K–12 Alignment

Use this chart to determine the best question stems for your different groups of students.

★	●	■	▲
Why was each text written?	For whom was each text written? Why?	Describe the purpose and audience of each text. Cite specific details from the text in your response.	Compare and contrast the purpose and audience of each text. Cite specific details from each text in your response.
What is the message of each text?	How are the central messages of the texts similar? How are they different?	Compare and contrast the central messages of the texts.	Compare and contrast the central messages of the texts. Explain how the central messages agree or conflict with each other.
How do the authors of the texts agree? How do they disagree?	On which points do the authors of the texts agree? On which points do they disagree?	Cite specific points where the authors agree and where the authors disagree.	Cite specific points in the texts where the authors agree and where they disagree. Use evidence from the texts to explain why they agree and disagree.
What does _____ (text A) tell about? What does _____ (text B) tell about?	How does _____ (text A) describe what happens in _____ (text B)?	How does _____ (text A) describe a cause? How does _____ (text B) describe the outcome/effect? Use evidence from the text to support your ideas.	Use textual evidence to explain how _____ (text A) describes the cause of an outcome/effect described in _____ (text B).
_____ (text B) tells about _____ (problem). How is it solved in _____ (text A)?	What solutions can be found in _____ (text A) to support the problem described in _____ (text B)?	Cite the solution(s) found in _____ (text A) for the problem(s) described in _____ (text B).	Use textual evidence to explain how _____ (text A) provides solution(s) to the problem(s) described in _____ (text B).

Connecting Texts K–12 Alignment (cont.)

★	●	■	▲
How are the ideas in _____ (text A) and _____ (text B) the same? How are they different?	In what ways do _____ (text A) and _____ (text B) describe the same ideas? In what ways do they describe different ideas?	Identify how _____ (text A) corroborates or refutes the idea(s) in _____ (text B). Use the texts to support your answer.	Use textual evidence to describe ways in which _____ (text A) corroborates or refutes the idea(s) in _____ (text B).
What details in _____ (text A) tell more about _____ (main idea in text B)?	How do details in _____ (text A) build on the main ideas in _____ (text B)?	Use textual evidence to show how details in _____ (text A) elaborate upon the main ideas in _____ (text B).	Identify textual evidence to explain how details in _____ (text A) elaborate upon the main ideas in _____ (text B).
What does each author think about _____ (event/concept)?	What is each author's opinion about _____ (event/concept)? How does this affect their descriptions?	Explain how each author's perspective influences how the events are described in each text.	Describe how the perspectives of each author are similar and different. Explain how this influences the ideas presented in each text.
Think about how each author tells about _____ (event/concept). How are they different?	Reread how each author describes _____ (event/concept). List ways in which their descriptions are different.	Analyze the retelling of _____ (event/concept) by each author. Describe the points that conflict with each other.	Analyze the retelling of _____ (event/concept) presented by each author. Explain where the accounts conflict with each other.
Do the texts have the same purpose/point of view? How do you know?	Describe how the texts have the same purpose/point of view/text structure.	How could the texts be grouped based on purpose/point of view/text structure?	Describe how the texts can be categorized based on purpose/point of view/text structure.

Answer Key

Answers will vary. Possible answers and sample answers are provided.

Honest Abe (page 13)

1. The author describes Lincoln as the 16th president, a hard worker, a good man, and an honest man.

2. The author wants us to know that Abraham Lincoln was an honest man who worked hard and told the truth. The text lists these qualities.

Dreaming of Freedom (page 15)

1. Example: The most important concept from Tubman's life is that she wanted all slaves to be free.

2. Example: The sentences that help me understand that Tubman was a brave woman are "Harriet risked her own life and her freedom for others," "She made 19 trips back to the South," and "She was a very brave woman."

Martin Luther King Jr. (page 17)

1. Key social studies words: *civil rights movement*, *freedom*, and *March on Washington for Jobs and Freedom*. There is also an image of Martin Luther King Jr. in front of the Washington Monument.

2. Key phrases include: "King was arrested and threatened," "He kept on marching and preaching," and "He was not worried about death."

George Washington (page 19)

1. Textual evidence includes: thousands died fighting, 17,000 died of diseases, the army barely survived the winter, and the war lasted eight years.

2. Example: The author wants the reader to understand that Washington fought through tough times and did not give up. Examples from the text include: "many opportunities for surrender presented themselves ... however, Washington inspired his troops and they persevered," and " ... although he was afraid to make mistakes, he took the position and worked diligently for the new country."

Government (page 25)

1. The text describes services as "for everyone."

2. Leaders and laws are connected because leaders make laws to keep people safe.

U.S. Constitution (page 27)

1. The main idea is that the U.S. Constitution is a set of laws that says how the U.S. government should work.

2. The key details include: it lists what Americans can do and should have, and it tells how the government should be split into three branches.

Electing Leaders (page 29)

1. Facts and examples include: voting, writing, speaking about their views, and joining organizations.

2. Examples include: citizens have a great deal of control through the ballot box, state and local elections are just as important as national ones, and that these decisions affect people's daily lives.

Impeaching a President (page 31)

1. Congress did not accept Johnson's explanation for why he fired Edwin Stanton. The significance of the order of events is that Johnson fired Stanton after Congress passed the Tenure of Office Act, which gave Congress grounds for impeachment.

2. The details in the last paragraph are factual. It is true that no president has ever been removed from office by impeachment. The paragraph doesn't say if they should or shouldn't have. It just states what happened.

Jobs Around Town (page 37)

1. We need people to do different jobs because some jobs provide services and others sell goods.

2. Words that help a reader understand what a good is are *treats* and *food*.

A Good Read (page 39)

1. The main events are Benjamin Franklin opened the first library, more libraries were opened that rented out books, and modern librarians do many things. The events in the text help create the message because they tell how modern libraries came to be.

Answer Key (cont.)

2. The term *library keepers* helps explain what the job of a librarian used to be because it explains that they take care of libraries.

Protecting the People (page 41)

1. Evidence includes: not all people who want to become police officers can handle the training, the exam to become a police officer is not easy, of the thousands of candidates, very few are invited to the academy, and even a traffic ticket can disqualify someone.

2. The conclusion helps a reader understand that police are specially trained and charged with the task of keeping the peace and protecting people.

ER Doctors (page 43)

1. The text describes how ER doctors encounter many unexpected situations. When first treating a patient they may diagnose based on symptoms. They also use test results to diagnose patients.

2. Example: The job of the ER doctor is complicated. They need to listen to symptoms to diagnose patients. They must also consider other pieces of the puzzle because symptoms can be misleading. Other examples where this would be true are for pediatricians and other types of doctors.

Being a Good Leader (page 49)

1. Example: A leader is fair and is a good example to others.

2. Example: Leaders do what is right and show others that they should also do the right thing.

Being a Good Citizen (page 51)

1. Example: The most important thing the author wants me to learn is that people have responsibilities at home and in their communities. By doing them, people are being good citizens.

2. Example: Being a good citizen relates to me because I have duties at home and in school.

Civic Responsibility (page 53)

1. Example: The key words *follow the laws*, *voting*, *serving on juries* and *holding public office* relate to my understanding of civic responsibility because they are examples of civic responsibilities.

2. Example: Civic responsibility relates to my community because each citizen has responsibilities to keep neighborhoods safe and strong.

What Can You Do? (page 55)

1. Example: President Kennedy wanted people to serve their country in times of peace. I obey the laws, but I could also start volunteering at a shelter.

2. The author's intent is to explain that people show their civic responsibility in other ways. Examples from the text include how people today help victims of national disasters.

Settling Down (page 61)

1. After the Nile River flooded, the water went down, there was new, rich soil, grasses and reeds grew, and ducks and geese made homes there.

2. Example: I now know when and why people settled along the Nile River.

Ancient Egypt (page 63)

1. Example: The image of the pharaoh and the detail that he was seen as a god help me infer that the pharaoh was feared and respected.

2. Because the pharaoh was seen as a god, people had to do what he said without question. The reader can infer this because the text states, "When he spoke, his words became law."

Artistic Monuments (page 65)

1. Some key information about how pyramids were built that is missing from the text is how the workers were able to move such heavy stones up and down the ramps and how they were able to fit them together so precisely.

2. A possible conclusion is that many people were required to build the pyramids.

Answer Key (cont.)

How Did They Do That? (page 67)

1. The author provides details about how large the Sphinx is, how it is part lion, and how it symbolizes strength.

2. A reader may draw conclusions such as: ancient Egyptians put great effort into building monuments and tombs such as the Sphinx, it must have taken many people to build it, and this was possible because there was adequate food production.

Immigrants (page 73)

1. When immigrants leave their homes, they come to the United States, work hard, and hope to achieve the American dream.

2. Immigrants and their new neighbors could tell about immigration.

European Immigration (page 75)

1. If an immigrant was sick or had been in jail, the inspector could refuse to allow him or her into the United States, and that could split up a family.

2. Example: I could write it as an immigrant passing through Ellis Island and waiting to find out if my entire family would be allowed to come to the United States.

Asian Immigration (page 77)

1. Chinese immigrants had to escape from their homeland and weren't given the same opportunities as other workers. Americans didn't welcome people who looked differently and paid them less or didn't hire them at all.

2. Example: Immigrants from countries that also immigrated in the 1800s were not mentioned. These immigrants may have been jealous that the Chinese immigrants were able to work together and form communities.

Welcome to the United States (page 79)

1. An inspector's decision was life changing for an immigrant. It could force an immigrant to return to his or her homeland, or it could allow him or her access to a new life in the United States.

2. If an inspector determined that an immigrant was sick, he or she was not allowed into the United States. However, if an inspector decided that an immigrant met all the qualifications, then he or she was allowed to start a new life in the United States.

China (page 85)

1. Jobs that are the same today include farmers and workers who make things such as dishes and pots. Now, there are more people working in factories, and those goods are sent all over the world.

2. Before, Chinese people lived in the Yellow River Valley on farms. Now, they still live there, and they also live in big cities.

Ancient China (page 87)

1. Before the Shang Dynasty came to power, Chinese people didn't trade much with other countries. Large mountains separated people. They grew crops, made silk, and made clay dishes and pots.

2. After the Shang Dynasty came to power, they began to make tools and wheels, they worked with bronze, and they began to write.

Communist Takeover (page 89)

1. China and its people were hopeful prior to the civil war. The country had been ruled by dynasties for over 2,000 years. The people wanted everyone to work together to do what was best for the country. They wanted the government to own the land and pay everyone equal wages so there wouldn't be rich and poor people.

2. Example: The positive impact of communism is that it got rid of dynasties that had ruled for over 2,000 years. The negative impacts of communism are that many people were killed, and more than 20 million people starved to death.

China's Population (page 91)

1. Causes include: the population was growing too quickly, the country was getting too crowded, the population was overwhelming social services, and China didn't have the natural resources to support such a large population.

Answer Key (cont.)

2. The positive effects of China's one-child policy is that it helped reduce the population to a size that could be supported by the land. The negative effects were that a single child had to support two parents and four grandparents as they aged, there were not as many workers to help on family farms, and families took drastic measures to ensure male children.

Greece (page 97)

1. Greeks long ago and people today both want to understand the world and learn about the things around them.

2. Example: Greeks long ago and people today are alike. The text says that people still live in Greece, and they wanted to learn like people today do.

Ancient Greek Language (page 99)

1. Both the ancient Greek alphabet and the English alphabet have vowels and consonants. Both alphabets use mostly straight lines to write letters.

2. The Greek alphabet has 24 letters, and the English alphabet has 26 letters.

Ancient Greek Education (page 101)

1. Education in ancient Greece is different from today because it was not required, only rich families could afford it, only boys attended to school, and students wrote on wax-covered tablets. It is similar to school today because students were taught to read, write, and count.

2. In ancient Greece, boys were taught to read, write, recite poetry, and play instruments. They were also taught trades in apprenticeships. Girls learned to spin and weave at home. If their families could afford a tutor or their mothers could teach them, then the girls could learn to read and write, too.

Greek Influence (page 103)

1. Example: Hippocrates, Aristarchus, and Eratosthenes all made contributions to the field of science.

2. Example: Aristotle contributed to several branches of scientific study, whereas Pythagoras was a mathematician who worked out a famous theorem about triangles. Aristotle's ideas had the greatest impact on the world because he "started several areas of scientific study."

Exploring New Places (page 109)

1. Explorers went to new places they did not know because they wanted to be rich, they wanted to find gold, and rulers wanted more land.

2. Kings and queens paid for the trips because they thought the men would bring back gold and make them wealthier. They also hoped to gain more land.

The Journey of Lewis and Clark (page 111)

1. Example: It was a good decision for Jefferson to hire Lewis to lead the expedition because Lewis and his team learned a lot about the places they traveled.

2. Lewis and Clark recorded the weather, made maps, and wrote and drew pictures about new plants and animals.

A Path to the Pacific (page 113)

1. Example: Lewis and Clark kept detailed journals during their trip containing maps and descriptions of new plants and animals. This helped because the journals were full of new and useful information.

2. Criteria include: the journals were full of useful information, Lewis and Clark claimed land for the United States, and the country became larger and wealthier as a result of their exploration and resulting discoveries.

Magellan's Trip Around the World (page 115)

1. The problem Magellan faced was that the Pacific Ocean was vaster than he could imagine, the crew was starving, and many died or left the expedition. He urged the crew to continue and as a result, many of the men died in conflicts with islanders and many more died from starvation and disease.

Answer Key (cont.)

2. Example: Magellan was a determined explorer. This was both a strength and a weakness. His crew was able to circumnavigate the world and discovered a western sea route to the Spice Islands, but many of his crew died along the way because he convinced them to persevere rather than turn around to get home safely.

Mapping a Town (page 121)

1. The map shows where various places are in a town.

2. The key on the map tells where homes, stores, schools, churches, parks, the zoo, hospitals, and city hall are located.

Food in the United States (page 123)

1. The symbols help the reader identify where each type of agriculture comes from in the United States.

2. The reader may infer that some states do not have much agriculture while others have many different kinds of food grown there.

1783 New World Map (page 125)

1. This map relates to European colonization in the 1700s because it shows Spanish colonies in the Caribbean and the newly formed United States, which were British colonies.

2. The reader may infer that Europeans explored the Caribbean and eastern North America extensively since there is much detail. However, beyond the Mississippi River, little exploration had been done.

Colonial Savannah (page 127)

1. The reader may infer that colonists had both cleared the land and planned the community before beginning to build. This can be concluded because there are dense trees all around, and the buildings are lined up in neat rows.

2. The map illustrates the changes in Savannah across time because you can see that there is a cluster of buildings in the middle that look finished and some in the front that look like they are partially complete. There are also plots of land that look like they will eventually be built upon.

Washing Dishes (page 133)

1. The setting is a home kitchen.

2. The people are a woman and a girl who are working together to do the dishes.

Flag Day (page 135)

1. The words in the image help the viewer understand that this poster was made to celebrate the 140th Flag Day and what the flag represents.

2. Example: This image was created to remind people to celebrate Flag Day on June 14th. I know because the poster lists the date of Flag Day.

War Poster (page 137)

1. There are words above and below the eagle. They help the viewer understand that the artist wants people to buy war savings stamps.

2. The eagle symbolizes the United States, and the airplanes represent its enemies during World War I.

Election Day (page 139)

1. This image may help the viewer understand that some people saw women's suffrage as gender-role reversal.

2. The phrase "Election Day" helps the viewer understand the setting of the political cartoon. The phrase "votes for women" helps the viewer understand the artist's message.

Voting (page 145)

1. Example: The message in the first text is that there are rules for voting. The message in the second text is that voting is important.

2. Example: The author of the first text thinks that voting keeps things fair because each person gets to vote once. The author of the second text thinks that voting is important because it helps both the community and the country.

Answer Key (cont.)

Choosing Leaders (page 147)

1. Both texts explain that voting is important. They are different because the first text explains how voting takes place and the role children can take, while the second text explains that voting shows a commitment to the world around you.

2. The details in the first text build upon the main idea of the quote because they explain how voting shows a commitment. The details also explain that people can vote honestly because ballots are kept secret, and therefore, people can vote what they truly think.

How Do We Vote? (page 149)

1. In the first text, the audience is people who want to understand the history of voting and in what ways votes are counted, such as with special cards or digital booths. The audience for the second text is citizens who want to know that their vote is given as much weight as people in positions of power.

Electing the President (page 151)

1. The first text explains how voting for president has changed with new types of campaigning and media, such as television. The audience is people who want to learn the history of how voting has changed. The second text is for people who understand the essential role of a sacrament, and the text's purpose is to convince people to vote. Both texts express the idea that voting is a responsibility of citizens.

2. The quote by Theodore Hesburgh corroborates the first text because it explains that how candidates present themselves plays a big role in how citizens vote. If candidates are able to get people excited about and interested in voting for candidates, then it leads to a more involved democracy.

Notes